AUSSIE OUTBACK

The second book in the Tess's Tours Series

Tess's Tours

Aussie Outback

Sue Towler

Author's Note

Whenever someone asks me what the most memorable tour was during my 15 years as a tour operator and tour guide, I never hesitate to say – this one – THE FLINDERS AND BIRDSVILLE TOUR. When I look back on it, I often wonder how we got away with it and survived.

This is a true story, however, in order to protect the privacy of the travellers and everyone involved with this trip, the characters are fictional and in no way are they meant to portray any person or persons living or otherwise. This trip took place fourteen years ago so much of the narrative is improvised but it reflects the essence of the people and conversations that were had at the time.

Other Books By This Author

Elizabeth's Diaries
Brigit
Isolation
Sounds Bad
Nellie
NZ's Wild West Coast (Tess Tours)

Website: sue-towler.com

Facebook: www.facebook.com/susy.co.nz

Cover Photo by Sue Towler – Cameron Corner, Australia

Table Of Contents

The large doors slid open as Tess approached them with her luggage trolley. She ventured tentatively through into the Arrivals Hall of the Adelaide Airport with her thirteen Kiwi Senior passengers in tow and looked around for a sign with her name on it. She had no trouble spotting the tall heavily bearded man with long white hair holding his sign aloft. His hair was tied back at the nape of his neck, his pleasant face sporting a wide grin; not what Tess was expecting but she felt immediately at ease.

'Hi, I'm Tess,' she said holding out her hand and looking up at the smiling face, 'are you Jack?

'Nope, I'm Slim, Jack is back at the office, I do the shuttle runs,' he grinned at her taking her hand.

'Are you our driver for the trip?'

'Nope again, Bill is your man for that. He's just done a trip to Tassie so he's having a few days off, he'll be picking you up tomorrow morning. Everybody here then?' he asked glancing around at the group.

Tess turned and counted heads - again. She was always counting heads.

'Yes, that's us,' she said, 'thirteen pax plus me.'

'Hi everyone, welcome to Adelaide,' Slim smiled at the group, 'grab your bags and follow me.' He led them outside to a waiting 17-seater shuttle. The group climbed aboard while Slim stowed the suitcases in the luggage trailer hooked on behind. He climbed into the driver's seat, pulled out his logbook and, turning to Tess sitting in the passenger's seat beside him, said, 'Comfort Inn, is that right?'

'Yes,' said Tess.

'Now do you want the direct route or the scenic one?

'Any difference in the price?' Tess grinned back.

'None whatsoever,' he said with a twinkle in his eye.

'The scenic route it is then,' Tess started to laugh. She turned to her passengers and said, 'Slim is taking us on a scenic tour of the city so stay tuned, I have no doubt he will have plenty to show us and talk about.'

Slim put on his headset and drove out of the airport carpark, shoving his exit card into the gate machine with practiced ease. He showed them a wonderful variety of interesting and historic sites, including statues of people he knew they would probably recognise, and beautiful tree filled parks with streams running through them. Eventually he pulled up at St Peter's Cathedral and asked if they would like to get out and have a look inside.

'It's one of our much-admired landmarks,' he said proudly.

They meandered quietly and reverently through the majestic interior, eyes roaming skyward taking in the magnificence of the building's structure. When they got back in the van, Slim drove them through the main shopping centre pointing out some of the historic buildings and popular shops, including the well-known Haigh's Chocolate Shop, before heading to their motel for the night.

By the time they pulled up outside reception at the Comfort Inn, Slim had everyone in the palm of his hand. He was the consummate entertainer, he'd had them in hysterics within a very short time of leaving the airport, and they were still chuckling when they climbed off the van. He unloaded the suitcases and stacked them outside on the footpath under the portico, while Tess went to check in at reception. When she came back with the keys and rooming list, Slim was about to head off so she said goodbye to him and thanked him profusely for the most fun ride from any airport she'd ever had.

'Wish you were our tour driver on this trip,' she said hopefully.

'Wish I was too, unfortunately my tour driving days are over now, getting a bit too long in the tooth for long trips these days,' he said sadly. 'I enjoy doing the shuttle work though, keeps me out of mischief, well almost. Enjoy your trip everyone, Bill is a very experienced driver, you will be in good hands.'

Tess got her travellers settled into their rooms with instructions to fill out their breakfast request forms for the next morning and hand them in to reception on their way to dinner. When she got to her own room, she put the jug on to make coffee, ironed a fresh shirt and put it in the wardrobe for the morning then sat down to check for any missed phone calls or emails. Even though her phone now indicated that she was switched over to Telstra, she wasn't sure how far into the Outback the signal would reach. There would be times, possibly days, when there was no signal at all. She hoped Bill carried a satellite phone on the bus in case there were any emergencies, her passengers were all seniors, any number of things that could go wrong with them, especially health-wise.

Tess had a bit of reorganising and repacking to do now that the flight was over. She took a day bag out of her suitcase to carry all the things she would need with her on the bus during the day, thinks like her water bottle, insect repellent, sunscreen, hairbrush, deodorant, peppermints, a couple of snack bars, compact mirror, lip balm, tissues, disinfectant wipes, facial wet wipes, sachets of her favourite coffee, wallet, notebook, phone, and a couple of pens. She went through her briefcase to make sure she had all the paperwork she needed for the rest of the trip, the return airline tickets and pick up list could now be packed away in her suitcase. She filled her briefcase with guidebooks and maps and checked she had plenty of paper and pens. After repacking her suitcase, Tess made a coffee using one of her own sachets, she hated motel coffee. She placed the steaming cup down on the bedside table, piled a couple of pillows up against the headboard, sat on the bed with her feet up and relaxed back on the pillows, letting out a deep sigh of satisfaction. She was finally back in Australia, a country she loved almost as much as her beloved New Zealand, especially the Outback. She was really excited about this trip, except for the fact that she was still a little nervous about meeting her driver for the first time.

It was raining when Tess made her way across to the motel dining room that evening, but it didn't seem to have dampened her travellers' spirits at all, they were too excited to be worrying about a bit of rain. Tess knew it would be warmer and drier the further north they went, she was looking forward to it, especially after the cold wintry weather they had been experiencing back home.

Day 2 – Adelaide to Port Augusta

It was still raining the next morning when the bus arrived at the motel to pick them up. Tess went out to meet the driver, he looked older than she thought he'd be but considering where they were going, she decided that maybe that was a good thing. The stocky grey-haired man greeted her with a broad smile.

'Morning, you must be Tess, I'm Bill, your driver for this intrepid tour of yours.'

'Hi Bill,' Tess held out her hand, 'nice to meet you.'

Bill glanced around and spotted a pile of suitcases lined up outside reception. 'These yours?' he asked.

'Yes, I hope they are all there, should be fourteen suitcases and some day bags.'

Bill opened the door of the trailer that was hitched to the back of the 22-seater Hino bus and began loading the bags.

'Would prefer they take these on the bus,' he said dropping the day bags to one side,' there's plenty of room.'

Tess nodded and went back to her room to brush her teeth. She applied lipstick, checked her appearance in the long mirror on the wardrobe door, piled last-minute items, including her two cameras, into her day bag and slung it over her shoulder, grabbed her briefcase and walked out the door pulling it closed behind her. She glanced up at the cloudy sky, took a deep breath and letting it out slowly decided, 'I'm ready.' She put her day bag and briefcase on the front seat of the bus and glanced back at the passenger seats. The bus was an old one, the seats looked comfortable enough, but it certainly wasn't flash. The passengers were gathering outside the bus so she asked them to collect their day bags from beside the trailer and pop them under their seats. As they began to climb on board, one of the passengers said in a loud voice, 'Oh, are we going all that way in this?'

Bill popped his head up from stowing the suitcases in the trailer and responded.

'Where we're going madam, this little beastie will do the job. The last thing you want to be driving in the outback is some namby-pamby computerised vehicle that is going to sigh and turn itself off at the slightest inconvenience. Those corrugated dirt roads out there are a bitch, you need something that can cope with that, something you can fix with a spanner, not a computer.' He glanced around at the less than enthusiastic faces. 'Look, did you come here to cruise up the highways, or did you come here for an adventure, because I can assure you, an adventure is what you will have.'

Tess smiled gratefully at Bill and turned to her group.

'Bill is right, if you are here to cruise the highways in a flash bus you are on the wrong trip. You are welcome to stay here and catch a flight back home if you wish, I will make the arrangements for you. You have all read through the itinerary, you should have some idea of what to expect, so if you want to see the real Outback of Australia in all its goddam glory then I suggest you get yourselves on that bus.' She gave them what she hoped was a confident smile. Thankfully they smiled back, sucked up their concerns, and got on the bus.

Once everyone was on board Tess did a head count as Bill climbed into his seat and started the engine. She introduced him formally to the group so he turned in his seat and gave them a warm welcoming smile.

'Welcome to the land of blue skies, red dirt and blow flies,' he laughed. 'I only got my bus licence last week but as we are driving mainly on dirt roads and not busy highways, I should be okay.' There was a spattering of laughter. He turned further round in his seat and looked directly at his passengers. 'Sorry about the lecture before,' he said, 'but I would rather clear the air and start off on a good footing, than let things fester. Look, I know this old girl isn't like those big tour buses you see cruising around, but trust me, where we're going, they wouldn't last five minutes. I spent several years driving long-haul trucks through the Outback, I know what I'm talking about.'

Doug spoke up, 'I for one have never been in the Outback, that's why I came. I'm definitely up for an adventure, and if this old girl is up to the task, then so are we.' He looked around at the rest of the passengers. 'I think I speak for the rest of us, don't I?'

Everyone nodded their assent.

'I see you have a television set mounted up there,' commented Jack, 'I guess that's so we can watch the footy?'

'I doubt we'd get any reception where we're going,' smiled Bill, 'and to be honest, I don't even think it goes. So, is everyone happy?' There were a few nods of heads and some 'yes's'. 'Righty-oh then, let's get on the road,' said Bill jovially, as he turned back in his seat and put the bus in gear.

Tess leaned across to Bill and asked, 'Have you seen the itinerary?'

'Sure have, wouldn't be much of a driver if I didn't pre-plan a trip now would I?'

'I don't know,' she confessed, 'I'm not used to working with drivers I've never met before or had time to sit down and go over the details with.'

'Don't worry,' he smiled, 'we can go over everything tonight after dinner if you like?'

Tess sighed with relief; her gut instinct was telling her she was in good hands. The passengers chatted noisily as they headed out of the city.

'Adelaide reminds me very much of Christchurch,' said June as she took in the architecture of the tall buildings.

'I was thinking the same thing,' said her sister. 'Great minds.'

'Slim took us for a drive around the city yesterday,' said Jan.

'Did he now,' laughed Bill, 'still fancies himself as a tour guide does he.'

'Actually, he was very good,' added Tess, 'he had us in fits of laughter most of the time.'

'Yes, he was an excellent tour driver in his younger days,' admitted Bill.

They left the city boundaries and headed into the more remote parts of the state. When Tess spotted the Gungellan Pub in Freeling just north of Gawler she let out a squeal of delight.

'That's the pub that was featured in the *McLeod's Daughters* TV series,' she said in explanation. 'We've gotta go in and have a look.'

Bill laughed at Tess's enthusiasm; how could he refuse. Most of the passengers knew about McLeod's Daughters because the TV series was still playing in New Zealand at the time. They were eager to go in and take photos and be able to say they had *'been there, done that'* to their friends and family when they got back home. Tess bought herself a sleeveless jacket with the *Gungellan Pub, McLeod's Daughter's* logo on it, she was stoked.

From Freeling they carried on up through the wheat fields of the Gilbert Valley and the wine region of the Clare Valley. They pulled into a rest area with toilets and picnic tables for morning tea. Bill opened a small door at the back of the bus and took out the morning tea box and thermoses that he'd stowed in a space behind the back seats. Tess helped him set up while the others went to the loo or took in their surroundings. They had left the rain behind for now, the sky was still cloudy but at least it wasn't as cold as it was back in New Zealand.

'Do you think it will be like this for the rest of the trip?' asked June, glaring at the clouds. I was hoping for sunshine and blue skies.

'Me too,' responded Tess, 'I'm well over the winter back home and it's only August,' she laughed.

'I brought my own sachets of coffee with me, hope you don't mind,' June added guiltily as she lined up to get some hot water.

'Not at all, I do the same,' Tess confided.

As they got back on board the bus, Samantha said, 'I read somewhere that there are a lot of deadly animals and insects in Australia.'

Tess waited until everyone was seated before she responded.

'Yes, there are certainly a lot of interesting creatures lurking about but to be honest, I haven't come across anything to be too alarmed about in my travels,' she looked to Bill for some support.

'They are more scared of us than we are of them,' he began. 'Most of them tend to stay clear of well-travelled and populated areas, but having said that, I would advise you all to be very aware of your surroundings when we are out in the open like this, especially at these roadside rest areas. Always wear shoes outdoors and watch out for snakes, especially in long grass and roadside verges. I have seen snakes and goannas crossing the road in front of me when I've been driving on tours. If we do spot anything interesting I would ask that you stay on the bus, for their sake and your own. Last thing we want to do is cause distress to the creatures by getting too close to them, but I will endeavour to get as close as we safely can so you can get a good look and take photos.'

The group nodded their understanding of the instructions. Tess and Bill took their seats and they were off again. They travelled on to Port Augusta where they cruised around the town looking for suitable cafes for lunch. Bill stopped at a central point in town and dropped everyone off. They bustled away in twos and fours looking for food or just browsing the shops. Tess and Bill walked together to a nearby café and, after ordering lunch at the counter, sat down at a small table in the corner.

'Seem to be a nice bunch,' said Bill.

'Yes, so far so good,' agreed Tess. 'So Wadlata is next on the list and then out to the jetty before we head to the motel, are you okay with that or do you know of other places we could visit?'

Bill smiled. 'There's a hundred and one places I could take you to Tess, but it would take more than a few hours. There's bound to be many places we could visit at any one stop, but when you are travelling and limited for time you can only do so much, as I am sure you are well aware.'

Tess agreed. 'If you know of any attractions, other than the ones listed on the itinerary, that you think might be a better fit for the group, please don't hesitate to tell me about it Bill, I value your local knowledge and experience, after all I am a Kiwi not an Aussie.' She flashed him a grin and he laughed.

'Thanks Tess, I appreciate you including me, I will go through the list tonight and see what you've got.

After lunch, everyone piled back on the bus and Bill drove them the short distance around to the Wadlata Outback Centre. Tess got out and stood in the stairwell of the bus to address the group.

'This place is amazing from what I've heard,' she said indicating the building at the end of the carpark. 'Take your time, we have all afternoon, we'll meet back in the Tuckerbox Cafe at the front of the building and once everyone is there we will head to the motel.'

Tess was keen to have a look through the Museum, she had heard so much about it from one of her friends who had stayed in Port Augusta a few years ago. Once everyone was off the bus, she waited while Bill locked it, and they walked in together.

'You ever been through here Bill?'
'No I haven't, I'm looking forward to it.'

They walked through the doors and stepped into another world. Once inside it was clear that they were going to be drawn in different directions, so they agreed to follow their own path and meet back at the café. Tess wandered around, stopping to watch videos of wild animals living in the Outback and listening to conversations between landowners about what it is like living in such remote places and in such harsh conditions. She came across a small room with a couple of rows of seats and a very large screen. As soon as she sat down the screen came to life and she was transported back millions of years in time. She watched enthralled, as images of evolution and transition unfolded in front of her. The timelapse video showed the changes in the creation of Australia from millions of years ago to what it is today. Tess was surprised to learn that when the Australian Continent first broke away from East Gondwana, not only was New Zealand still attached to it, she knew that much, but that Antarctica was as well. She marvelled at the part where much of inland Australia had once been under water for quite some time before drying out and becoming the vast desert country it is today. It appeared that the continent underwent a lot of climatic changes over millions of years with rainfalls becoming less and less frequent.

She was still sitting in total awe when the lights came back on. It wasn't until someone sat down beside her that she came back to reality and left the room to wander around the next lot of exhibits. She loved everything about the Outback, the stories, the artifacts, the history. She was becoming more and more excited about this trip and if these exhibits were anything to go by, it was going to be amazing. When she finally made her way out to the Tuckerbox Café an hour later, Bill was sitting at a table by the window reading a newspaper. Several of the passengers were sitting at other tables enjoying a cuppa and chatting about what they had seen, while others browsed in the adjacent gift shop. She ordered a coffee and sat down at Bill's table.

'What did you think?' Bill asked looking up.

'Loved it,' said Tess beaming, 'especially that time lapse video going back millions of years, that really blew me away. What about you?'

'I think the highlight for me was the stories about the early settlers, why they came here and why they are still here. I was intrigued with the aboriginal stories too, sort of puts everything into perspective, doesn't it?'

Tess nodded. 'Sure does.'

Did you see the story of Tom Kruse, the Birdsville Mailman?' Bill asked.

'I did, what an amazing character, and man what a ride that must have been, battling your way over sand dunes to deliver the mail and supplies to outback station owners.'

'Keep it in mind, I will tell you more about it when we get to Maree.'

Tess made a mental note but figured it probably wouldn't be necessary, she knew Bill would most likely remember to tell the story when he was ready.

Tess waited until everyone had returned to the café before directing them back out to the bus. Bill drove out to the Port Augusta jetty where most of the group took the opportunity to go for a walk along the iconic structure. From there, they drove around to the motel and checked in, allowing plenty of time for a refreshing swim in the pool or a cup of tea and a lie down before dinner. Those who still had some energy left, went for a walk down the street to the main shopping area.

About half an hour before dinner, Tess went to the bar and found Bill waiting there. He bought her a drink, and they went and sat down in a couple of armchairs to chat.

'With regards to the commentary,' Tess began hesitantly, 'obviously I have never been in the Outback before, but I have done some research and I have made some notes and I've got some brochures about the areas we are going to. How well do you know about where we are going?'

Bill leaned down and took a notebook from a bag on the floor beside him.

'Tess, if you would like me to do the commentary, I would be happy to.' He flicked through the pages of his notebook. 'As you already know, I spent several years as an Outback trucker and I used to jot down notes about my experiences on the road. I had no idea what I was going to do with it but when Jack offered me a job driving his tour buses, it came in very handy. I am more than happy to do the talking, I consider a bus load of passengers my captive audience,' he said with a twinkle in his eye.

Tess was relieved. 'I don't mind doing commentary about places I know,' she said,' but this is one time I feel totally out of my depth. Thanks again Bill, you're a gem.'

'My pleasure,' he said.

'I'll be able to concentrate on taking photos and doing the video,' said Tess, 'that's quite a big job in itself.'

Dinner was a selection of chicken or beef dishes with tiramisu, fruit salad and ice cream for dessert. A couple of the travellers stayed behind in the bar after dinner to chat, while the rest traipsed wearily off to their beds.

Day 3 – Port Augusta to Wilpena

Tess was the last to arrive at breakfast the next morning, everyone else was already sitting at the table eating when she walked in at seven thirty. She said good morning to Bill as he passed her in the corridor, he was heading out to stow the bags in the trailer.

'Morning everyone, have you all put your suitcases outside your doors or in the foyer?' Tess asked.

There was a chorus of acknowledgements then one or two hopped up and went to do just that. 'Thank you,' she said.

She turned and walked over to the coffee machine and popped some wholemeal bread into the toaster. The bacon and eggs looked tempting but she decided against it. She tended to eat far too much when she was on tour and would invariably groan at the scales when she got home to find she had put on a couple of kilos. Happened every damn time. She went over and sat down with the two ladies from Christchurch, they were sisters. June had been a regular traveller on Tess's tours but this was the first time her sister had travelled outside New Zealand and she had been a bit anxious about it.

'Morning Aggie, how are you this morning, did you sleep well?'

'I did, yes, thank you,' she mumbled through a mouthful of toast. 'Now that I'm here and I've met everyone I am feeling much better about the whole thing.'

'Good to hear,' smiled Tess, relieved. 'How about you June, have a good night?'

'Yep, you know me Tess, up and at it and ready for anything,' she laughed.

An hour later they were loaded up, the motel account paid, and they were off, right on time. Bill looked across and smiled at Tess.

'Gonna be a good day,' he said, 'I can feel it in me bones.'

'Hope you're right,' said Tess. She threw her camera strap around her neck, held her video camera on her lap and settled back in her seat, looking forward to filming the ever-changing landscape ahead of them. They drove around the sights of Port Augusta for a while then headed away from the Spencer Gulf into the foothills of the Flinders Ranges.

'Home of the Flinders Council and about a thousand people,' Bill said as they slowed down and cruised through the small outback town of Quorn.

About 40kms north of Quorn, Bill pulled off at a signpost pointing to the Kanyak Homestead at Tess's request. 'I hear this place has an interesting history,' she said to Bill.

'Yes it does, do you have some notes on it?'

'I do,' said Tess pulling a folder from her briefcase. 'The tour company who set this trip up for me, sent notes on some of the places they recommended we visit, and this is one of them.'

As they pulled up at the homestead site Tess turned in her seat to address her passengers.

'This is the Historic Kanyak Homestead site, let's get out and have a look. There is some information on a board over there, but I will tell you more about it when we get out. Tess waited until everyone had gathered around the information board then added to the story.

'Kanyak Station was taken over from the Aboriginal Barnggarla people and turned into a cattle station in 1852 by Hugh Proby. The area is very dry, so it was tragic, and probably a bit ironic, that twenty-four-year-old Proby downed while crossing the swollen Willochra Creek, while he was trying to herd a mob of cattle during a thunderstorm, apparently, he was swept off his horse. There were several subsequent owners, in particular John Randall Phillips, who helped to build the station up to become one of the largest in the district with seventy families living and working here.'

'Phew,' said Gus, 'it was tough enough running a farm with just our family, let alone running a station this size and looking after all those families as well.'

Tess continued. 'Those weren't his only difficulties, Gus. Because they were so remote, the station had to be self-sufficient. They had a large homestead, cottages for the workers, workshops, huts, and sheds which were all mostly built from local stone as there was a limited supply of timber. The station, at some stage, switched from cattle to sheep but they also had cows, pigs and vegetable gardens, and they even had their own cemetery.'

'There's a place similar to this just out of Christchurch,' offered Jenny.

'Ah, you're talking about Longbeach Estate,' said June, 'Yes I've been there, it's a wonderful historic place, and you are right, a similar concept but on a smaller scale.'

Tess left the group to wander around the ruins while she went off on her own to take photos and video.

They travelled on to Hawker and decided to stop there for lunch. Bill pulled up outside the roadhouse, the bus doors opened, and everyone piled out into the heat of the midday sun, making their way inside. Once they put their orders in, they went outside to sit at the large wooden picnic tables under the wide veranda. Country music was blaring from an outside speaker and when *Acky Breaky Heart* came on, some of them got up and did a line dance, encouraging Tess to join in. They took their time over lunch, there was no real hurry today. Tess walked around with her cameras clicking and videoing to her hearts content. When they finally reboarded the bus, Bill took them for a drive through the town showing them the old Hawker Hotel.

They travelled the short distance to the Castle Rock Lookout where Tess and a couple of the passengers got out, the others were content to stay inside in the warmth of the bus, it was getting overcast and windy again. Apart from the odd bit of snoring now and again, the rest of the trip to Wilpena was relatively quiet. Tess was disappointed some of them were missing the fascinating changes in the terrain, but she reminded herself that this was just the beginning of their sojourn through the Outback, and that there would be plenty more opportunities to see the desert terrain in the days to come. Bill woke them up with some commentary as they drove through the National Park.

'The Ikara-Flinders National Park covers 95,000 acres of rugged, ancient mountain landscapes,' he said. 'The gorges are tranquil places with lots of trees and home to a variety of wildlife that come and go with the seasons.'

They pulled into the Wilpena Resort carpark and Tess jumped out to go and check in at reception. She came back with the rooming list and directed everyone to their rooms once they had collected their suitcases.

'Your keys are in the door, dinner is at six thirty tonight, breakfast from seven in the morning. I will fill you in on tomorrow's events at dinner this evening.'

'Is there a bar here?' asked Harvey.

'Yes, it's down there by the dining room,' Tess pointed down the hall to her right. 'Your rooms are down this way,' she indicated the corridor running in the opposite direction, 'so you shouldn't get lost,' she added with a grin.

Tess let herself into her room, threw her suitcase on the bed, unpacked some fresh clothes and had a quick shower to freshen up. She went through her notes then headed down to the bar to catch up with Bill. As they were sitting chatting Tess felt someone staring at her and turned to see a man smiling at her. She was a bit annoyed because he was sitting with his arm around a woman's shoulders. She swung back and faced the bar.

'Bloody men,' she hissed through her teeth. Bill looked at the group sitting around the lounge.

'What's up?'

She told him about the guy smiling at her. He looked around and said, 'Well he's coming over.'

'What!' She turned back and watched the man approaching then relaxed and smiled. It was a relation of hers from back home. 'Hi, gosh haven't seen you for ages,' said Tess, 'what on earth are you doing way out here?'

'Could ask you the same thing,' he said.

'I'm here with a tour group, this is my driver, Bill.

'Nice to meet you,' said Bill, then turning to Tess he said, 'Look why don't I go and get everyone seated for dinner while you guys have a catch up.'

'Thanks Bill,' Tess said gratefully, 'that would be great.'

Tess and her cousin talked for a while, catching up on all the family 'gos', before Tess excused herself and said she needed to join her group. 'It's been great seeing you though, we should catch up again when we get home.'

Tess went and sat down at the table and called for everyone's attention.

'You can have a leisurely breakfast tomorrow morning,' she said. 'At nine o'clock we will be heading off on a little adventure, a picnic lunch will be provided. Now, I think seven of you wanted to go for a flight over the Pound tomorrow afternoon, has anyone changed their minds? I will need to let reception know if you have.' She waited while they talked amongst themselves then pulled a piece of paper out of her folder and read off the names of those who had indicated their wish to do the flight when they booked to come on the trip.

June put her hand up. 'If there's room, Aggie and I would like to go please. Aggie wasn't sure when we booked but she would like to go now, wouldn't you Ag's?'

Aggie nodded. 'I don't want to put anyone out though,' she said hesitantly.

'I will go and see if they can fit another two on,' said Tess, 'so you other seven are all good to go then?' They all nodded. 'Nobody else?'

When there was no response from the others Tess got up and went to reception to see if they could get another two people on the flights.

'You are in luck,' said the receptionist, 'a couple coming from Adelaide have been delayed so their seats are available, sold to you,' she smiled. 'Do you have the names of the others who are going, just to make sure we have everyone?'

Tess told the girl the names of the other seven passengers. 'And yourself of course,' she said brightly.

'Oh, I hadn't planned....' Tess began.

'It's complimentary for the hostess and driver,' she confirmed. 'Sorry did nobody tell you that. I have eleven spaces in all, that includes you and your driver.'

Tess hesitated for a moment. 'They might have said but I didn't give it much thought. Thank you, I would love to go. I will just go and check with my driver to make sure he wants to go too.'

She raced back to the table and spoke quietly to Bill so no one else could hear.

'We have been offered complimentary flights over the Pound tomorrow, do you want to go?'

'That would be great,' he said, 'I would love to go, thank you.'

'Don't thank me, thank the operators,' she laughed and went back to inform the receptionist that all eleven passengers would be there.'

Once the group left the dining room, Tess sat with Bill in the lounge and discussed the following day's tour around Wilpena and Gum Creek Station.

Day 4 – Wilpena Pound and Gum Creek Station

Tess caught up with Bill at breakfast and let him know that Les, their guide for the Wilpena and Gum Creek Station tour would meet them at reception at 9am.

Everyone was on board the bus by the allotted time. Bill was filling out his logbook while Les jumped on board the bus and perched himself on the engine mound between the two front seats facing the passengers.

'Mornin' everyone,' he said brightly, 'my name's Les. I understand you are from across the ditch is that right?'

'Yes,' they all responded.

'Well I won't hold that against ya,' he chuckled. Now my station is called Gum Creek, for obvious reasons as you will see. I will get Bill to drive you around Wilpena then we'll head on out to my property and park up by the creek where we will have a picnic lunch and a cup of billy tea. Anyone here had billy tea before?'

A couple of the passengers raised their hands.

'Well, the rest of you are in for a treat,' he said. 'What time are your flights this afternoon?' he asked, leaning back to talk to Tess.

'We have to be at the airstrip by two thirty she said.'

'Okay, I will work in with that. We can have lunch around midday, that will get you back to the resort by one thirty. It's only a twenty-minute drive out to the strip.'

For the next two hours they drove around the Wilpena area visiting the Aroona Homestead ruins alongside the ABC ranges, and Blinman, where they stopped to take in the beauty of the Parachilna Gorge. From there they drove on to Gum Creek station.

'What's that railway line over there?' asked Jack.

'That's the old Ghan line,' explained Les. 'The old Ghan stopped running back in the early 1900's. The Ghan train that's running today goes from Adelaide right through to Darwin.'

Bill followed Les's directions and they turned off onto a small dirt track through some trees to a creek.

'This is our lunch stop,' announced Les. 'There's a long-drop toilet just up that track there behind the trees if anyone needs it.'

Les set about lighting a fire while Tess and Bill sorted out the lunch. By the time everyone had gathered back at the bus, the fire was roaring and two blackened billies filled with water had been placed on a metal grill sitting on top of the flames.

Once the filled rolls, fruit cake. Mugs, milk and sugar were set out on an old wooden table, Les went over and threw a couple of handfuls of black tea leaves into the boiling water in one of the billies. He let it boil for a minute or so then took it off the fire using a stick through the handle and set it down on the ground. He added a little cold water, which he explained to those standing around watching in fascination, 'helps the tea leaves to settle down to the bottom.' He tapped the side of the pot a couple of times with the stick then proceeded to fill the tin mugs lined up on the table.

'Help yourselves,' he called out, 'there's milk and sugar there if you want it. The other billie is just plain boiling water for any coffee drinkers.' He stood back with Tess and Bill and watched as everyone grabbed a filled roll and a mug off the table.

'Mmm, this is delicious,' Sam said as she waved her roll at Les. Thank you.'

'Now that is a mighty fine cup of tea,' confessed Gus. 'Reminds me of my hay-making days when Mandy used to bring strong black tea in a bottle over to the paddock for us.'

'It sure is tasty' added Lena, 'best I've had in a long time. I wonder what my neighbours would say if I built a fire in my backyard to make billy tea.'

Everyone laughed, then silence reigned as they sat and ate their lunch, enjoying their peaceful surroundings, occasional bird songs, and the gentle murmur of the river. Tess took photos of them all sitting around enjoying their lunch.

'Delicious fruit cake,' commented June.

'Sounds like you have some fans,' laughed Tess. 'Thank you Les this has been great. it's things like this that really make a trip that much more special.'

'You're welcome Tess.'

They said their goodbyes to Les when they dropped him off and made their way back to Wilpena Resort. Tess turned around to talk to the passengers before they disembarked.

'Those of you flying this afternoon will need to be back here by two o'clock. The rest of you are free to wander around the compound, there's a delightful little souvenir shop over the road there and a café. If you are wandering around, please stay on the pathways and keep an eye out for snakes and wild animals.'

The group of eleven arrived out at the airstrip just before two thirty and were ushered into a small building where they were briefed on flight procedures and asked to sign disclaimer forms. Two identical planes sat on the tarmac. The young pilots came in and introduced themselves.

'Afternoon everyone, I'm Patrick and this is Jackson. How many have we got?'

'Eleven,' said the girl behind the counter.

'Great. Where are you all from?'

'New Zealand,' responded Tess.

'Kiwis eh, I'm heading over there for a skiing holiday in a couple of weeks. Which ski field would you recommend?'

'That would depend on which island you want to go to,' said June. 'My recommendation would be Cardrona or Coronet Peak if you want to head down to Queenstown.'

'There's nothing wrong with Ruapehu,' said Mandy defensively.

Patrick laughed and held up his hands. 'I don't want to start a turf war,' he laughed. 'To be honest I have already booked my tickets to Queenstown so Coronet Peak or Cardrona it is.'

'Gosh,' said Jenny, you lads look hardly old enough to shave.' She hadn't expected the pilots to be so young.

'We do find older folk have concerns about our age,' he laughed, 'but I am 28 and my buddy Jackson here is 26. We spend time at places like this flying small aircraft to build up our hours, we are both training to become commercial pilots.'

'Which airline do you want to fly for?' asked Harvey.

'That depends on who will hire us,' laughed Jackson, 'our preference would be Qantas of course. Now, let's get you all on board. We will take six in one plane and five in the other. We will need to balance you out weight-wise so if you stand with the group you wish to fly with, we will do our best to keep you in that group.

Who are the hostess and driver?' asked one of the pilots.

Bill and Tess raised their hands. 'Good we will decide which flights you will be on if that's okay.' They both nodded.

It took some time to get everyone on board the small aircraft. Space was at a premium and some of the taller or larger built passengers had difficulty manipulating their less than co-operative limbs to get into their seats. Once everyone was strapped in, they taxied down the runway and became airborne. The views from the air were breath-taking, they hadn't expected to see so many mountain ranges spreading way out into the distance. As they flew around, they could see each other's planes, it put things into perspective in respect of the vastness of their surroundings. The pilots gave running commentaries as they flew over different areas, the most exciting of which was the 'Pound' itself.

'The Aboriginal Adnyamathanha name for the Pound is Ikara, which means, "meeting place", the surrounding mountains form a natural amphitheatre. As you can probably see, it is right in the heart of the Ikara-Flinders Ranges National Park. Many people tried to farm it over the years but for the past forty or fifty years it has been run as a tourist resort. People started visiting here around 1945, and that's when the tourism ideas started to form.'

When they landed and climbed their way out of their planes the group excitedly exchanged experiences. Tess thanked the Pilots while Bill went off to bring the bus around from the car park. The excited banter continued as they climbed on board and made their way back to the resort. When everyone had left the bus and gone inside, Tess looked across at Bill and said, 'Thank you for today, it's been fabulous.'

'My pleasure Tess and thank you for the flight, something I've always wanted to do. Another thing to cross off the bucket list.'

'So how long is this bucket list of yours?'

'Getting shorter by the day,' he chuckled, see you at dinner. Wonder if you will be meeting any more long-lost relatives tonight?'

Tess laughed, 'It's a small world, you just never know do you.'

Day 5 – Wilpena to Arkaroola

The group were up bright and early the next morning, eager to begin their day. Tess was running late because of the time spent at reception going through the account and she had to pick up the packed lunches she'd ordered the night before. She made her way out to the waiting bus with the lunches, packed them in the back then went back for her briefcase and cameras and climbed in to the passenger's seat.

'Sorry to keep you waiting,' she apologised, turning in her seat to look at her passengers as they headed out of the resort compound, 'hope you all had a good night's sleep.' They nodded and she continued. 'We are heading further into the mighty Flinders Ranges today, as you will already know. We will travel through Blinman again and the Chambers Gorge then on to Arkaroola where we stay for the next two nights. I think you will be pleasantly surprised by the terrain there; it is quite something. Any questions?'

'Yes,' piped up Jack from the back seat, 'Why are they called Flinders Ranges if the area is predominantly Aboriginal?'

Tess glanced across at Bill hoping like hell he had the answer. He did an eye roll, smiled, then tapped the side of his nose with his forefinger. She sighed with relief, yes, he did. Bill pulled the headset down off the hook beside his head, flipped open his notebook on the dashboard and began to enlighten the passengers.

'That's a very good question Jack. You will have noticed that most of the names of the places here-abouts are Aboriginal names. But, with regard to these particular ranges, apparently Governor Gawler named them back in 1839 after an early explorer. The Aboriginal name is Ikara. Some local people refer to the ranges as Ikara-Flinders National Park. The range runs for about 430kms starting at Port Pirie and ending at Lake Callabonna.

'Quite an impressive range then,' said Jack. Does this area have one particular tribe, like the Maori tribes back home have their own areas?'

'Yes, the tribe that inhabits this area,' he paused for a moment, 'look, I will spell it out for you because I'm not sure how to pronounce it properly. It's A-d-n-y-a-m-a-t-h-a-n-h-a.'

A couple of the passengers quickly wrote the name down as Bill spelled it out and the next few kilometres were spent trying to pronounce it.

'Tell you what,' offered Bill helpfully, 'why

don't we just ask them when we get to Arkaroola, I'm sure they will be only too happy to tell us their history. In fact,' he glanced at Tess, 'you will be doing the four-wheel drive excursion I take it?'

'Yes,' said Tess, 'that's the highlight of the next two days there.'

'Good, they will tell you everything you need to know about the whole area.' He pulled over to the side of the road and turned to the group. 'Anyone want to stretch their legs and take in this impressive landscape?'

He didn't need to ask twice. As soon as the coach door opened, they bundled out and stood in awe of the breath-taking vastness and beauty that stretched out before them right across to the impressive ranges that ran along the horizon.

'I thought our Alpine Range down South was impressive, said Aggie, 'but this is quite something isn't it?'

'I think both are impressive in their own unique ways,' Tess responded, 'just vastly different. Probably as opposite as you can get.'

'True,' agreed Aggie.'

Some of the group made their way down the rocky slope beside the road in search of flora and fauna. They didn't have to look too hard; the area was awash with a variety of wildflowers and plants they had never seen the likes of back home in New Zealand.

'What birds and animals should we be on the lookout for Bill? June had a brightly coloured pamphlet in her hands depicting a variety of Australian wildlife.

'What does it say in your booklet there?' asked Bill.

'It's got lovely photos of all the wildlife, but not where they all live.'

Bill reached out for the pamphlet and glanced through it.

'Well, for starters, the yellow-footed rock wallaby, and this Wallaroo and these Big Red Kangaroos all live in the Flinders National Park area. As for the birds, I will have to check my notes but from memory I think you could expect to see the more common parrots, galahs cockatoos and corellas. And old man Emu of course. He glanced further through the pamphlet. 'Ah, yes, the wee desert mouse, but you would be lucky to see one of those from the side of the road. As for the reptiles, let's have a look. Hmm, yes, you might be lucky enough to see a bearded dragon, we sometimes see them on the road, along with a snake or two. Another fascinating little character we might be fortunate enough to see is the wee Echidna. Delightful little thing.'

'Thanks Bill,' said June, glancing through her pamphlet again, trying to remember all the ones Bill had just pointed out to her. 'I'll let the others know,' and she wandered off.

Tess didn't hurry them along. Despite the fact that it was still quite breezy, they were rugged up for it, and time was on their side.

They drove into Blinman, found a public toilet with a picnic table nearby and set up for morning tea.

'That winds a bit brisk,' Tess remarked. 'Hope we don't have this for too much longer, better than rain though I suppose.'

'God, I could murder a coffee,' said Sam sidling up to Tess,' didn't sleep well last night.'

'You okay?' asked Tess, concerned.

'Yeah, I'm okay, just sometimes I can't turn my jolly old brain off,' she laughed. 'Spent last night dreaming about strange creatures peering at me from the undergrowth and Kangaroos fighting each other.'

Tess raised an eyebrow at her. 'Must have been quite a dream.'

'Yeah, it was.' Sam took her coffee from Tess, gave her a wink and wandered off.

Tess watched Sam as she walked away, not sure what to make of her.

'Cup of tea for me please Tess,' and her thoughts were diverted to her next customer.

As they stood around taking in the small peaceful settlement, Bill spoke up.

'This place, Blinman, is the highest town in South Australia, and believe it or not, it has a huge population of around twenty people.'

Everyone laughed.

'Haven't seen anyone yet,' said Jack.

'Guess you wouldn't get away with doing anything naughty in this place,' said Sam, 'eeeeverybody would know about it before it even happened.'

That brought forth more giggles.

'It's basically just a small service place for the surrounding rural sector,' continued Bill. 'It used to be a thriving mining town of around 1500 people in its heyday. Now though, there's just the general store down there, a post office and the hotel with visitor accommodation and a restaurant.'

'What were they mining?' asked Gus.

'Copper,' replied Bill simply. 'Right, if everyone has finished their drinks, let's get packed up.'

They arrived at the Arkaroola Tourist Village by early afternoon and went straight into the dining room for lunch. Tess went to reception to book in, collect the rooms keys and rooming list and confirm mealtimes.

'Dinner at six thirty tonight and breakfast starts at seven in the morning, is that correct?' asked the receptionist.

'Yes, that works for us,' said Tess. 'Do we get a choice of meals or how does it work?'

'We have a-la-carte and blackboard specials,' the receptionist explained.

'Perfect,' said Tess, 'that definitely suits us. Is it a cooked or continental breakfast?'

'Cooked. I see you're all going on the Ridgetop Tour first thing tomorrow. Morning tea is included but make sure they take their cameras and a bottle of water. It's an amazing trip. And I see you are booked in for a guided bush walk this afternoon.'

'Yes,' said Tess, 'what time does that start and where do we meet?'

'Meet in the dining room at two o'clock and we will take it from there,' said the receptionist.

Tess wandered into the dining room to hand out the room keys and pass on the information. 'Take the time to have a look around,' she said, 'there is a room just out front here filled with gemstones that have been found in the Flinders area, well worth the look if you're into that sort of thing. Our Ridgetop tour takes off at eight thirty in the morning so we need to be at reception by no later than eight fifteen. Everyone good? I will see you all at two then.'

Tess decided to go and unpack and get settled then go and have a look at the gemstones before the bush walk. She was surprised to find such a variety. She recognised the more common ones, quartz, amethyst, aquamarine but there were many she had never heard of. Mona wandered in and came up to stand beside Tess.

'I would never have thought you would find all these gems way out here,' said Mona, leaning over one of the glass cabinets. 'Look at this, cornwallite, it looks like emerald.'

'I was thinking the same thing, Mona. 'Look at the colours in this one, kulanite, and this gorgeous bright pink one, flouromins. That magnetite is an interesting looking piece too.'

'Of course, with you living in Waihi, you would have seen plenty of quartz before, said Mona.

'Yes, that's one advantage of living in a gold mining area I guess,' smiled Tess, 'but I have never seen quartz like this one before, it looks like caramel candy.'

'So it does,' laughed Mona.

They moved silently through the rest of the gem displays oohing and aahing over the various pieces before heading off to join the others for the bush walk.

Day 6 – Arkaroola and Flinders Ranges

The group were all ready and waiting outside reception by eight thirty when two purpose-built four-wheel drive land-cruisers and their drivers turned up to take them on the adventurous trek into the Flinders Ranges. Bench seats ran down either side of the open cab at the back of the vehicle allowing clear viewing all around. It was still a bit breezy with a bit of a chill in the air but the skies were clear. The passengers had been advised to rug up warmly as they would be travelling in open vehicles, and it would also be a little cooler on top of the ranges.

Once the pre-trip briefing was over, the troops climbed up the fold-down steps into the back of the vehicles and settled themselves side by side along the bench seats, excited about what this day might bring. Some felt a little bit nervous and out of their comfort zone, while others relished the promise of another adventure. Leaving a few minutes distance between them, the vehicles took off up the dirt track and climbed up to their first stop, a wooden platform erected in such a way as to afford a birds-eye view over the entire compound below.

'This is Coulthard's Lookout,' explained the driver. 'The area you see spread out before you, is part of the Arkaroola Wilderness Sanctuary. It was a sheep station overrun by sheep, camels, donkeys, rabbits and dingoes before the Sprigg family bought it in the 1960's and made it what it is today. The government is threatening to sell off uranium mining rights on this land but there is a fair bit of opposition to that so it will remain to be seen if it goes ahead.'

'Why is this called Coulthard's Lookout. Who are the Coulthard's?' asked June.

'Adnyamathanha people,' the guide explained, they are very passionate about preserving and protecting the land.'

As the group looked down on the compound below, they were surprised to see how many more buildings there were than the just the accommodation and reception buildings they had already seen. This operation was bigger than they realised. Leaving the platform, they headed up hill and down dale through the vast barren terrain past dried, wizened, stick-like trees and the occasional clumps of unusual plants.

'Those plants look like someone's hiding behind them with a spear,' laughed Sam.

The driver agreed and added that the plant

was, 'a Xanthorrhoea Australis, otherwise known as the grass tree, or blackboy. The Aboriginals call them bukkup, baggup or kawee.'

The drivers in both vehicles ran an ongoing commentary as they manoeuvred their vehicles up and over the rough narrow dirt tracks trying to avoid the ruts. At times, the passengers had to hang on to the sides of the vehicle or the metal frame above their heads to stop themselves from falling out of their seats. Eventually the vehicles headed towards a steep hill with a bit of a track running up to the top of it. There didn't appear to be a lot of space at the top, so the passengers weren't expecting to go up there. They became a tad nervous when the drivers began to drive up the steep, rutted track.

'Hold on,' they called to their alarmed passengers. At the top there was just enough room to park two vehicles. They carefully manoeuvred their vehicles one at a time and parked up. Once the passengers, some on shaky legs, climbed out of the vehicles, their nervousness was replaced with awe. A wooden picnic table had been set up in a clear space amongst the rocks behind the vehicles.

'Welcome to Sillers Lookout,' one of the drivers said with a big grin on his face.

The magnificent scenery stretched out before them as far as the eye could see. The passengers, coffee mugs in hand stood around the edges of the peak and just gazed in awe at what lay before them. Tess took dozens of photos and got some wonderful video footage as well.

'We'll be travelling through that area over there in the coming days,' explained Bill, indicating an area way off in the distance.

They were reluctant to leave when the drivers asked everyone to get back into their vehicles. This had been the perfect climax to a pretty amazing day. They were weary by the time they got back to the compound, but they were also blown away by the day's excursion. It had proved to be way more than they had expected.

Day 7 –Arkaroola to Marree via Leigh Creek

Rain had been reported in the area they were heading to and Bill was concerned that the clay roads might be getting a bit sticky. He'd phoned the manager at the Maree Hotel the previous night.

'Gidday mate, had much rain out your way lately?'

'Nah mate, we don't get rain out here,' drawled the hotel owner, a smile in his voice.

'Just wonderin' about those clay roads,' queried Bill. 'Don't want to get ourselves stuck out there.'

'And where would the harm be in that?' laughed the hotel owner 'Not a bad place to get stuck in, we've got plenty of beer on tap and food in the chiller, we're all good.' He let out a raspy laugh. 'Nah all good here mate. See ya when ya get here, I'll shout you a beer,' he added before hanging up.

Bill hadn't said anything to Tess about the call, but he still had his doubts about the weather.

He knew there had been talk of rain but apparently none had made its way as far as Maree, and he hadn't heard anything to the contrary, yet.

The passengers and their luggage were loaded up and ready to go by eight o'clock after a substantial cooked breakfast in the dining room. Tess picked up the packed lunches and stowed them in the back of the bus. Everyone was excited and buzzing with anticipation about the next leg of their journey, which would take them further into the Outback of Australia.

'I'm really looking forward to this part of the trip,' Jack said to Samantha as they boarded the bus.

'Why this particular part?' asked Samantha, curiously.

'I don't know, it's just the thought of being so far away from civilisation and being at the mercy of the desert,' he smiled. 'I read a book once, called 'See Australia and Die,' he added with a laugh.

'Oh, that must have been comforting,' Samantha said sarcastically.

Jack laughed at her reaction. 'Actually, it was a bit of an eye-opener, but damned interesting all the same. It was a bunch of stories about people who died or had near misses from the elements and animals and such.'

Samantha shuddered, 'Great, that's really got my confidence up – not,' she said snarkily.

'Don't be like that Sam,' Jack pleaded.

'Nothing like that is going to happen to us, we are in good hands here, it's not like we are out there in the wilderness on our own like some of the stories I read about.'

'What sort of things happened to them?' Sam's curiosity got the better of her.

'Well, there were those who got lost in the desert and wandered off instead of staying with their vehicles. A lot of them died but some actually survived, mostly by sheer luck or by following the rules.'

'What rules?' asked Sam.

'Telling someone your plans, taking plenty of water with you, staying with your vehicle if you get stuck or break down, that sort of thing.'

'Oh yeah, guess that's logical.'

'Not to some people it's not,' replied Jack with a shake of his head. 'People can be pretty ignorant sometimes when it comes to travelling alone in remote areas.'

'So, what are some of the other ways to 'Die in Australia,' smiled Sam, using her fingers to form quotation marks.

'There was quite a variety of incidents in the book actually.' He thought for a moment then continued. 'It's not only the desert that people get lost in, there's also the bush that's full of nasties, like dingoes.'

Samantha shuddered.

'And in the water too of course, both places aren't the safest spots in New Zealand either to be fair and some of them were the sorts of things that could happen in any country. But then there's the crocodiles and the poisonous snakes and spiders and...'

Samantha put her hand up. 'I've heard enough, thanks Jack, that was very enlightening.'

'Well, you asked me to tell you about it,' retorted Jack, a bit put out. He turned and looked out the window, Sam turned the other way and chatted with Lena across the aisle, looking for a distraction from the thoughts Jack's words had conjured up in her mind.

Long straight corrugated red dirt roads disappeared into the distance in front of them, and wide-open landscape featuring tortured, stunted black trees stretched out either side of them for as far as the eye could see. Every now and then someone would exclaim, 'Look, there's an emu,' or 'Kangaroo on the right.'

They stopped on the side of the road adjacent to Moolawatana Station and set up for morning tea. They felt like they were in the middle of nowhere.

'This station has had such a variety of owners and changes of land boundaries over the years, they call it the 'Skeleton Block' because of all the area it has lost,' said Bill. He flicked over a page of his notebook. 'William Warwick bought the land in 1853 along with Holowiliena Station, Hamilton Creek ran through the property. Moolawatana was then bought and sold and added to and chopped about by several subsequent owners. It went from sheep to cattle in 1993 because of the constant dog attacks on the sheep. In that year, 1993, they shot over nine hundred dogs, ninety-eight of those were inside the dog fence. They had some pretty good rains in 1997 but unfortunately this was followed by a long dry spell causing a drought. There were some heavy thunderstorms in 2001 and then a locust strike. Apparently, it took two hours for the swarm of locusts to fly past the house.

'Ugh,' said Lena, 'imagine that it must have been terrifying.'

'I suspect it was,' agreed Bill. He looked up at the gathering grey clouds overhead. 'With any luck they may get some much-needed rain very shortly. Best we get packed up and on our way.

They crossed through the dog fence gateways a couple of times and had only seen two vehicles in the past three hours, the travellers were beginning to understand just how remote they were now.

'Is there anyone out there?' said Lena plaintively.

'I was thinking the same thing,' said Jan, 'with all this having to open and close gates business, it feels like we are on someone's private property.

Bill chuckled to himself, he knew the feeling well. He pulled off to the side of the road and let the passengers get out and stretch their legs. It was still overcast but no sign of rain yet.

Lena let out a squeal of delight as they wandered around on the deserted barren roadside.

'Look at this gorgeous wee beetle, it's bright

green, have you ever seen the likes of it?' Some of the interested group stooped over the beetle with cameras focused as it made its way up a sand dune oblivious to its audience.

They got back on the bus and carried on down the corrugated track. Suddenly, out of the blue, four vehicles appeared over to their left.

'There must be a road going across in front of us up ahead,' said Jack.

'There is,' affirmed Bill, we'll be turning on to it shortly.

'Looks like a drilling rig on that first truck,' said Gus.

'That second one looks like a water truck,' added Harvey.

'That'll be the supervisor and the boss in the other two vehicles,' laughed Sam.

'Probably the crew,' added Doug. 'They're certainly not wasting any time are they?'

'No speed limits out here I suppose,' said Harvey.

By the time they got to the crossroads the vehicles were well out of sight to their right. The signpost standing directly in front of them pointed right 264 kilometres to Innamincka and left 191 kilometres to Lyndhurst. They turned left on to the Strzelecki track and headed towards Lyndhurst.

'Must be a truck or something coming towards us going by that dust cloud,' exclaimed Harvey.'

'It is,' said Bill, 'think we'll just pull over here and wait until he's gone past.'

Everyone watched in fascination as the dust cloud rolled closer revealing only the front of the truck. As it drew alongside, the driver of the long truck and two trailer unit gave Bill a grateful blast on his horn, Bill waved back. He sat and waited for a few moments until the dust died down before pulling back out onto the track.

Just out of Lyndhurst, Bill pulled up at a small roadside stall.

'Come and meet Talc Alf,' he called out to everyone. 'He's a bit of a legend around here.' They piled off the bus and ventured in and around the rough-hewn wooden structure that housed Alf's talc sculptures and a blackboard and notice boards outlining his many ruminations and philosophies on life in Australia.

'Afternoon everyone,' Alf greeted the group with a big smile that peeked out from within his big unkempt bushy grey beard. Mandy noticed the twinkle in his eye and smiled up at him.

'Where are you from,' she asked, were you born in Australia? I detect a slight accent.'

'I was born in Holland ma'am,' he said brightly. My name is Cornelius Johan Alferink but everybody calls me Alf or Talc Alf, pleasure to meet you. Where are you folk from?'

'New Zealand,' they choroused.

'Welcome to the Land of the Golden Sun,' he said, pulling a small sculpture out of his pocket. 'Here let me explain how that name came about.'

The group stood in a semi-circle around Alf as he explained the meaning of the word Australia, when it was broken down into parts. Some were convinced it was true, others were a bit sceptical, but they enjoyed the story anyway. Alf continued talking as questions were fired at him from all sides. He was in his element, talking to people and sharing his ideas and philosophies on life, this was his way of life and he loved it.

In answer to a question, he responded, 'I travelled around quite a bit before I found what I considered to be the best talc deposit in Australia, Mount Fitton in the Flinders Ranges. I used to deliver the mail up there and then I'd come back home with a load of talc.

'So, is that where we get our talcum powder from? asked Mandy.

'Not necessarily from Mount Fritton, there are several mines around but yes, your talcum powder is initially mined and comes out looking like this,' he produced some samples and handed them around. 'I don't use talcum powder myself,' he grinned, 'but it's perfect for my artwork.'

There was a lot of excited chatter as everyone got back on the bus, some with purchases clutched in their hands. As they left, it began to rain.

Bill pulled up at the petrol bowser in Lyndhurst and filled up while the passengers got out and made their way into the roadhouse for lunch. Once they had had their fill, they moseyed on out to the bus and climbed aboard for the last leg of the days' journey.

'Not far to Maree,' announced Bill as they got underway. Turning to Tess he said, 'Looks like there's been quite a bit of rain through here. Road's a bit sticky in places.'

'Do you think it will be a problem?' asked Tess.

'Apart from the red clay building up on the tires and becoming slippery, no not really. At least not if this is all there is.'

Tess got the giggles.

'What's so funny,' Bill asked, a grin of amusement spreading across his face as he watched her.

'I was just imagining the clay building up on the tires until we were way up off the ground.'

'Bill laughed too. 'We'd be in trouble way before that happened. If the clay was that wet, we'd be sliding all over the place, damn stuff is like trying to drive on ice.'

'Have you ever done that?'

'What, drive on ice?'

Tess nodded.

'As a matter of fact, I have. I drove with some ice road truckers once, a long time ago. Not something I'd want to do again in a hurry though, scared the living daylights out of me. Give me the outback any day.'

They were on the outskirts of Marree now.

'Population in the Marree area is more than six hundred,' said Bill, 'seventy percent of them are men. About one hundred and fifty people live in the town, the rest are on the outskirts. The railway opened in 1884 and closed in 1987,' said Bill. 'There was a narrow-gauge line south of Marree which remained operational for freight traffic until the standard gauge rail line was completed. All trains north of Marree ceased when the new standard gauge line opened from Tarcoola to Alice Springs in 1980, replacing the Central Australia Railway in its role as the main line to Alice Springs.'

Bill drove on past the Hotel and did a tour around the town, stopping outside the Tom Kruse Museum. Tess turned around in her seat and asked if anyone wanted to get out and have a look through.

'Quite an interesting history,' she said. Once one or two made their way off the bus and headed into the building, the rest decided they might as well go in too, rather than just sit on the bus and wait.

'What's with the old truck there?' asked Gus

'That was one of the Birdsville mailman's trucks,' Bill responded. 'Has anyone heard of Tom Kruse? And no, I don't mean that Hollywood actor chap, I mean the Birdsville Mailman Tom Kruse.'

Frank said, 'Yes, a friend of mine loaned me a DVD about him, quite a story.'

'There's more info about him inside,' said Bill. They all traipsed in behind him.

'I've seen the movie too, and read about him over the years,' said Bill.

Bill proceeded to show everyone around the museum, he'd been here before and had found it fascinating and very informative.

'Here's a photo of one of the trucks loaded up with goods,' he explained, 'and that photo there is of another one of the trucks Tom used to deliver the mail. He took the business over from a chap named Harry Ding in 1948, Tom used to drive for Harry from about the age of 21.

The mail-runs had a fortnightly turn-around. The base radio stations at each stop would be abuzz with the news that 'Tom was on his way,' or 'Tom has arrived,' floating through the airwaves.

'Gosh it must have been exciting to see that truck arrive with supplies every two weeks when you lived in such isolation,' pondered Mona, 'I can't imagine what it would have been like to live so remotely, away from people and shops and everything.' Others agreed.

Bill stood back and let the group read the rest of the information for themselves. He smiled as the group split up and wandered around on their own in silence, reading and absorbing a fascinating time in history.

Once they were all back on the bus, Bill closed the door and drove off around the back of the hundred-year-old Marree Hotel. He pulled up in the middle of the yard out the back where there were several brand-new stand-alone motel units. From the back door of the hotel leading out to the rooms, large, flattened cardboard boxes had been laid on top of the wet clay for people to walk on. Bill did a bit of a chuckle. Tess glanced over at him.

He shrugged. 'Manager told me it never rains out here.' He leaned forward in his seat and peered out at the cardboard and the surrounding yard. 'Looks to me like they've had more than a light passing shower.' He and Tess both got out of the bus and before they headed towards the back door of the hotel Tess addressed the group.

'Stay on the bus until I get back, I'm not sure yet if we are out here or in the hotel.'

They plodded their way across the sea of cardboard and walked through the back door into a dark interior. The manager came out to greet them. He was a big bloke, tall and thickset with a rather serious expression on his face.

'Gidday Laurie, thought you said it never rain….'

'Don't even go there mate, just don't even bloody go there,' the manager interrupted, then a broad grin split his face and he laughed grabbing Bill by the hand pulling him into a bear hug.

Bill pulled out of the hug and turned to introduce Tess.

'Ah, the wee Kiwi chick, nice to meet ya,' he went to hug her but Tess stuck her hand out instead. He stepped back, took her hand and said, 'I don't bite love, despite what this bastard might have told ya.'

'So what's with all the cardboard out there?' asked Bill.

Okay, so we did have a bit of rain this mornin', that's just to stop everyone walking the red clay into the hotel and the motel rooms, it's a bitch to get off the carpet. The other thing is,' he looked apologetically at Tess, 'the rooms have only just been built.

We decided to put in cedar doors and the bloody things have swollen up so they don't shut properly. We have put hooks and loops on the inside to keep them closed so that will hopefully deter any would-be intruders.'

'Intruders?' gasped Tess, 'can we just stay in the hotel rooms instead?'

'Sorry love, we've been stripping the wallpaper and the rooms are all packed up. I'm sure you'll be fine, nothing to worry about.'

When Laurie had given Tess the rooming list, she gingerly made her way out through the mess of cardboard trying not to get any of the wet sticky mud on her shoes. She got everyone off the bus, explained that the doors had swollen up in the wet weather and that there was a latch inside the door to keep it shut. She was not about to tell them what Laurie had said about intruders. All she did say was, 'I know that doesn't seem very secure but if you are at all concerned just bang on the wall to alert your neighbour or yell out, okay?'

They all looked at each other, none of them too sure what to make of all this cardboard and insecure doors business, but Tess kept them busy by getting them settled into their rooms.

Bill came out, opened up the trailer and started removing the suitcases, some of the group were standing by ready to help.

'Sorry folks, they are a bit dusty,' Bill apologised, as he saw the state of the first two he pulled out. 'One of the hazards of travelling in the outback I'm afraid.' He turned to Tess. 'Might pay to see if you can round up some big plastic or polythene bags to put their suitcases in.'

'Where on earth am I going to find anything like that here?' she asked.

'There's a store across the road, you should find something there,' Bill muttered as he carried on hauling out the suitcases. When Tess got to her room, she used a small brush to get the dust off her bag and upon opening it, was dismayed to find the fine red dust had seeped inside her suitcase through the teeth of the zip. Bill was right, they needed to put their suitcases into plastic bags while they travelled on the outback bull dust roads. She looked at her watch and wondered what time the store closed. She had seen it when they drove in, and it was open then. She grabbed her wallet, did a mental count of the number of bags she would need and headed out across the dirt track, over the old railway lines and into the shop. Fortunately, they were still open.

'Hiya daarl,' drawled a voice,' Tess spun around but couldn't immediately see anyone until her eyes adjusted to the dim interior. She could see a rather plump but pleasant faced woman leaning on the counter watching her.

'Oh, Hi,' said Tess. I'm just looking for some large plastic bags, if you have any.'

'We have absolutely everything in this place,' smiled the woman. 'Names Rebecca, what's yours? You with that bus group that's just rolled in.'

'Yes, that's us. My name's Tess.' She reached out her hand, the woman ignored it and walked over to one of the shelves. 'For putting your suitcases in, am I right?'

'Yes,' replied Tess. Do you get many requests for them?'

'Yep, sure do. Best idea is to line the inside of your suitcase with one bag and seal all your clothes inside it, then put the whole suitcase in a second bag and secure that as best you can. Won't stop all the dust getting in but it will help.'

'Seriously?' gasped Tess. 'All that and it still

gets in?'

'Not from around here are ya daarl,' the woman drawled again with a chuckle. 'Guessin' you're from Kiwi land, am I right?'

'Yes,' sighed Tess, feeling a little out of her depth.

'S'alright daarl,' she said, 'I sell a lot of bags to unsuspectin' travellers, especially those with trailers. The front vehicle kicks up a fair amount of dust right into anything hooked on behind. Here, these are what you need. How many do you want?'

Tess took the roll of blue bags she was offered.

'There are fifteen suitcases all together.

'Right you are. She counted out thirty bags and rang the amount up on the till. Tess looked around the shop.

'Gosh, you really do have a big variety of stuff in here.'

'Yep, but only the stuff people really need, don't have room for no fancy bits and bobs. That all you need luv?'

Tess nodded and handed over the cash then, picking up the bags, she walked out of the shop and headed back to her room. She opened out one of the bags and checked the size perfect, the woman in the shop knew what she was talking about. She would take the bags to the dining room so everyone could grab a couple on their way back to their rooms after dinner. She glanced at her watch again, decided to have a shower after dinner, changed her top, ran a comb through her hair, checked her make up and went off in search of a nice cold drink. Bill was already at the bar deep in conversation with Laurie. Raucous laughter greeted her the minute she stepped through the door. She glanced around the lounge and saw most of the passengers sitting around talking amongst themselves. She wandered over to the bar to get a drink.

'This one's on me,' Laurie said amicably. 'Make up for the cardboard and the swollen doors, least I can do.'

'That is very generous of you,' said Tess, 'thank you.'

'What'll you have?'

'I could murder a long cold lemon lime and bitters please?'

'Comin right up.'

The evening was lively and convivial with lots of laughter and sharing of stories. Mona and Harvey felt comfortable enough to share the fact that they were not married and that this was the first time they had travelled together. 'We have been friends and neighbours for about fifteen years,' explained Mona, 'my husband died five years ago and Harvey's wife Mavis died two years ago and we have just been there for each other ever since.'

'You would be surprised how many times I've heard similar stories,' said Tess, 'it happens more often that you realise, where friends get together after their spouses die. And sometimes people meet up on a tour and stay together afterwards. Two of my travellers met on one of my tours and are now happily married.'

Jack looked across at Sam and gave her a wink. They had never met before this trip but they were getting along like a house on fire.

The conversation swung around to Australian birdlife, especially the ones with a very distinctive call that wakes you up first thing in the morning.

'If I wake up in the morning and I'm not sure where I am, the crows tell me I am in Australia,' laughed Tess. I love their cawing sound.

'Geez those galahs can kick up a merry din,' said Jack.

'The white cockatoos with the pink chests are the noisy ones I reckon, said Gus. No big flocks of birds like that back home.

'My sister lives in Western Australia and she reckons that everything in Aussie 'wants to kill ya', even the spearheaded grass,' said Lena. 'Don't know why anyone would want to live here. Apparently, the Kiwi kids that move here have to learn that they can't run around barefooted like they can in NZ and most of the houses are shut up with the air conditioning running all the time. I'd rather throw my windows open and let the fresh air and sunshine in. Most of the group agreed.

Just then the waitress came in to advise them that their meals were ready. They were served sumptuous plates of meat and vegetables followed by bowls of steamed pudding and custard or fruit salad. Nobody seemed to be in any hurry to go back to their rooms. Tess paid for the next round of drinks and the group carried on chatting happily, the staff even brought out complimentary cheese boards for them.

They were still chatting away as they headed to their rooms, seemingly no longer concerned about the sticky clay or their insecure bedroom doors.

Tess and Bill stayed on after everyone left and went over their plans for the next couple of days. Tess felt the next two days would be the most challenging ones of the whole trip, Bill agreed.

Day 8 – Maree to Birdsville

There was a murmuring of voices and the clinking of crockery and cutlery when Tess ventured into the dining room for breakfast the next morning. It appeared, once again, that she was the last one to arrive.

'Morning everyone, did you all sleep well?'

'We did,' they chorused.

'It's so quiet and peaceful out here, the silence is almost deafening,' smiled June. 'Best night's sleep I've had in ages.'

'Me too,' agreed Aggie. 'I feel like a box of fluffies this morning.'

'Did you manage to pack everything and seal it down tightly in your plastic bags?' Tess asked the group.

'Yes, we unpacked and lined the suitcases with one bag then repacked everything back into it as you suggested. We tucked the opening right down as tight as we could, then we put the suitcase inside the second plastic bag and tied a knot in it,' said June. 'Let's hope it works.'

'The lady in the shop said it might not stop all the dust, but it would definitely help,' said Tess.

'Are you kidding me?' queried Lena, 'that's unbelievable. Surely nothing can get through two lots of plastic bags.'

'I guess we'll find out when we get to Birdsville,' said Tess.

They left the hotel at around eight thirty under a clear blue sky.

'No sign of that rain now,' Bill commented to Tess, 'but that road still looks a bit sticky, hopefully it will dry out before too long and there's no issues ahead of us.' He put his headset on as they drove out of town.

'Morning folks, we are now on the Birdsville track. To our left, heading west is the Oodnadatta Track that will take you through Oodnadatta to Marla over in the Northwest. Now it's going to be a long day today so we will be taking short breaks for you to get out and stretch your legs. As you are all aware by now, there are no tar-sealed roads in the Outback. While most of it will be relatively smooth travelling, it certainly won't be like driving on tar-seal. There will be places where there is corrugation or deep tracks in the road some of it caused by the rain. It all depends on how long it has been since the grader has been through, and how much rain they've had. The good thing is, the rain that has just gone through will help to keep the dust down, for a little while anyway. We will be driving through the Tirari Desert,' continued Bill.

'Don't look for the sameness out here, look for the subtle changes in the landscape and the flora and fauna. The deserts offer a variety of sights you will not see anywhere else.'

They drove on in silence for a while, with the odd break out of conversation.

'Gosh, here comes a couple of cars,' said Mandy, 'must be peak hour,' she giggled.

'Looks like a four-wheel drive tag-a-long tour,' said Bill. 'You see them driving through the Outback from time to time. Sensible way to travel I reckon, at least you know there is someone on the other end of the radio to help if you run into any difficulties.'

'Looks like it's raining again,' said Aggie, disappointedly. 'I was hoping we'd seen the last of the rain.'

Bill glanced across at Tess. 'Let's hope we don't get too much more of this.' To the group he said, 'I can assure you there will be some very happy people out there celebrating this much-needed rain.

'If I was farming out here and hadn't seen rain for months or years at a time, I think I would be dancing naked in it,' laughed Gus. Mandy laughed and said she would probably join him.

They stopped at some old ruins just off to the side of the road where they took the opportunity to have a look around and stretch their legs. As they drove the next few kilometres, they passed through the dog fence once again and drove on towards the small settlement of Clayton.

'There's a suburb in Melbourne called Clayton,' said Jenny. I've got a friend whose mother lives there.'

'Look at that big puddle on the side of the road,' commented Harvey, they must have had a fair bit of rain here.'

'I think you'll find that's artesian water Harvey, it comes from underground.' Bill flicked open his notebook. 'For those of you who are interested, there is a massive underground source of fresh water right below us called the 'great artesian basin'. It covers an area from Cape York down to Dubbo, across to Coober Pedy and back up again to the Gulf of Carpentaria, an area of nearly two million square kilometres, it's been there for millions of years.'

There was a rustling of paper as some of the travellers got out their maps.

'That's a mighty big catchment of water,' exclaimed Gus.

'About a quarter of the size of the whole continent,' agreed Bill. 'That basin of water is the reason why Australia currently exists; it is the key to life in this area. Things would certainly be a lot different out here if it wasn't for that water.'

'How did it get there?' asked June.

'Good question,' said Bill flicking over a page in his notebook. 'It all started back when New Zealand was still attached to Australia and the land was called Gondwanaland. Basically, it's rain that fell over two million years ago. With all the earth changes over the past one hundred and forty million years, the ocean levels rose and fell. When things like ice ages and earthquakes happened, the water rose becoming trapped in the basin forming a sea. When the levels fell again the whole area became land once more. Some of you may have seen that time-lapse video about it back at the Wadlatta Centre in Port Augusta.'

Several of the passengers nodded their heads. They were listening intently, fascinated, wanting to learn more.

'The sea drained away leaving clay and silt deposits which formed into an impermeable stone. Rivers continued to flow for a time, carrying sand and gravel which formed a permeable sandstone, so, the water was trapped between solid rock at the bottom and a sandstone layer at the top which the water penetrated through, and it has been bubbling around below us ever since. The Aboriginals discovered it around 20,000 years ago, that's how they have survived out here in the desert for so long.'

'So how does it get to the surface?' asked Harvey.

'It comes up through bores that are drilled down through the rock. It's around three thousand metres deep in places and once the bore reaches it, it doesn't need to be pumped, it just flows up under pressure. The temperature of the water when it hits the surface ranges anywhere from around thirty to one hundred degrees centigrade. I heard that people from all over the world come to soak in these artesian waters, apparently it is full of minerals like calcium, magnesium, potassium, sulphur and bicarbonate. It has to go through cooling towers before we can drink it though.'

'I wouldn't mind a soak in a hot pool,' sighed Mona, my legs are giving me gyp.'

A couple of the others agreed with Mona, a soak in a mineral pool sounded like heaven.

'Sorry folks,' said Bill, 'maybe on another trip. We have places to go and people to see today.'

They drove on down the long straight red-dirt road through vast expanses of red desert which stretched from horizon to horizon, the barrenness only broken at times by the white sun-bleached bones of dead animals. There was a buzz of excitement when someone spotted a row of trees in the distance, suggesting that a settlement of some sort might lay ahead. There was, it turned out to be the homestead and compound of Etadunna Station. It was a large, well set up place with several sheds and houses. The passengers got out to stretch their legs but were back on the bus within a few minutes as it started to rain again. They carried on to Cooper Creek where they stopped for morning tea. The rain had stopped here so they wandered around swatting flies and paddling in the creek as they drank their morning tea and ate biscuits. Cooper Creek was a quiet peaceful spot with a camping ground close by.

'Wish we could bring the motorhome over and stay in places like this,' Jan said to Frank with a wishful sigh.

'Yeah, that'd be nice wouldn't it,' he responded.

Tess heard Bill start up the bus and hurried everyone along, they were reluctant to leave this place. As she settled herself down in her seat, Tess turned to Bill and thanked him for packing up the morning tea box.

'No problem,' he said, 'I could see you were enjoying yourself.'

Bill reached for his headset. 'Next stop will be the Mungerannie Roadhouse for lunch, a pie and a pint for lunch today,' he laughed.

'That'll do me just fine,' Doug called back.

Once they left Cooper Creek the landscape changed from red to white, although it was still vast and barren. As they travelled down one particularly desolate stretch of road, Tess suggested to Bill that he drop her off and go back up the road aways so she could video the bus travelling towards her, seemingly out of the middle of nowhere.

'I thought it might help to show the vastness of the desert,' she said.

'Good idea,' said Bill, 'here okay?'

'Yep,' said Tess as she prepared to exit. She hopped out with her two cameras slung around her neck and waved to the perplexed passengers as Bill turned around and went back up the road. She could only imagine how he would be explaining to the passengers what they were doing. She chuckled to herself and got her cameras ready to go. The bus disappeared into the distance just as a Peugeot car pulled up alongside her from the opposite direction.

'You okay there?' Two concerned male faces were peering intently at her and looking around to see if anyone else was about.

'Yes, I'm fine,' smiled Tess, 'I'm just waiting for a bus.'

The two men glanced at each other. Tess smiled, she could tell by the expressions on their faces that they thought they might have come across a crazy person.

She looked up and said, 'Oh, here it comes now.' She started the video.

The men, obviously relieved, both laughed and relaxed.

'So, what are you guys doing way out here?' she asked, as she focused the video camera.

'We're on our annual Peugeot run,' they said proudly. 'We do the three tracks, Birdsville, Strzelecki and Oodnadatta.'

'That's quite a trek,' Tess said. 'Well, have fun, my ride is here.'

They waved goodbye and carried on up the track.

As the bus got closer Tess carried on filming as Bill sailed on past. He drove up the road a short distance then turned back around to pick her up. She took more photos and video.

'What are they up to?' asked Bill, 'those people in the Peugeot?'

'Oh, they're on their annual run, there's a group of them apparently. Here's another couple coming towards us.

'They didn't give you any grief did they?'

'They thought they'd come across a crazy person for a minute or two, but no quite the opposite,' beamed Tess, 'they have given me an idea for another Outback tour. The Three Track Outback, the Birdsville, Strzelecki and Oodnadatta tracks. Could be quite an adventure,' she enthused.

Bill nodded and smiled at her excitement.

'Well, it will certainly give you something to think about.' He frowned as he looked out through the front windscreen and Tess turned to see what had caught his attention. There, right across the road in front of them was a deep puddle of water. Bill pulled up and got out to check the depth of the puddle to decide the best way to get through it. He got back on the bus and turned to the passengers.

'Any bags and things that are on the floor, you might want to put up on your knees,' he said. And get ready to raise your feet if you don't want to get your shoes wet.'

There was a gasp of alarm from the passengers then Bill laughed and said, 'only pulling your legs folks, we should get through this okay.'

He put the bus in gear and drove slowly and steadily through the puddle coming out the other side without any problem.

'What would you have done if we couldn't get through it?' asked Frank.

'I guess we would just have to sit here and wait until the sun dried it out or someone came along who could winch us through. Maybe one of those Peugeots,' laughed Bill.

As they got close to the Mulka Ruins, Bill asked Tess if she wanted to stop.

'Didn't know about them,' she confessed, 'sure why not. No doubt you know something about them,' she said cheekily.

'Course I do,' he smiled back.

As they pulled up alongside the ruins Bill suggested the passengers might like to get out and have a closer look. He would tell them a bit about the history of the place once they were standing out beside what was left of the once popular Mulka Store.

'George Aiston, a retired cop from Mungerannie, took over the Mulka Station in 1923 and by 1925 he'd built the Mulka Store, the remains of which lie hereabouts, and he put down a bore. It was the only store within a seventy thousand square mile radius, and he carried the biggest variety of stock you could imagine. George died in 1943 but his wife Mabel kept the store running until 1951. They certainly saw their fair share of huge dust storms and floods over the years.'

The next stretch of road was undulating sand dunes which provided a bit of relief from the straight flat dirt roads they had been travelling on.

'This is like riding a roller coaster,' laughed June as they breached the peak of another sand dune.

There was the odd chuckle from the passengers as they went up and over the sand dunes, all agreeing it was indeed similar to riding a roller coaster.

Eventually the bus pulled up in front of the Mungerannie Roadhouse and Hotel and the passengers disembarked eagerly, they were hungry and looking forward to lunch. It was still overcast and windy so most of them wasted no time getting inside. There were audible gasps of surprise as they walked in the door and saw the ceiling and walls bedecked in paraphernalia. Dozens of old Akubra slouch hats were pinned to the ceiling, and the walls were covered in photos, one area being designated to hundreds of business cards, pinned there by travellers from all over the world.

'Gidday folks, can I get you anything,' called the man behind the bar.

'We're here for lunch,' said Tess. 'I did phone ahead to let you know we were coming.'

A woman appeared from out the back. 'Tess?'

'Yes, that's me,' said Tess.

'Good on ya,' she said amiably. 'I'm all ready for ya. Go and find yourselves a seat in the dining room and I'll bring the food out. I've got a selection of small pies, toasties and fresh sandwiches. Bit of cake to have with your coffees afterwards as well.'

'Sounds great, thank you,' said Tess as she led the group to the café tables.

'Where are Jack and Harvey and Frank?' Tess asked looking around.

'Gone out to have a look at the old, rusted truck wrecks outside,' laughed Jenny. 'Typical blokes.'

'Did you see that truck and trailer unit out there loaded up with hay?' Gus said. 'What I wouldn't have given for a load like that when we needed it.' He saw the driver coming in through the front door and went over to have a chat.

Once the food came out the chatter died away and they ate in silence. When they finished eating, some of the group made their way outside to take a look around. There was an artesian hot pool out the back which drew their interest, especially as they had earlier been talking about the artesian water.

'Have we got time for a soak?' pleaded Mandy.

'Sorry Mandy,' not this time. 'If I ever do this trip again, I might add an overnight stop here.

It's lovely and peaceful isn't it,' she mused as she watched the flocks of birdlife either on the water or nestled along the banks of the creek.

Refreshed and eager to continue their adventure, the travellers climbed back aboard the bus. Bill had taken the opportunity to top up with fuel and Tess added another slab of water bottles to the boot.

'Good move,' said Bill, never miss a chance to keep your supplies topped up, you just never know how things are going to pan out in remote places like this.'

Back in her seat, Tess settled back with cameras at the ready, watching for anything of interest. There was a tinge of green along the roadsides now because of the recent rain and the terrain had gone from white back to red again. They went through large puddles on the road and the dirt track was becoming more corrugated and uncomfortable the further they went. Occasionally they would see stock grazing along the roadside.

'I would have thought those cows would be

frightened of traffic and keep far away from the road,' remarked Jan.

'Water runs off the road and feeds the plants along the roadside so there is often more food for the animals there than further inland,' responded Bill.

At one point Tess asked Bill to stop so they could get out and have a look at the wildflowers on the side of the road. The passengers were fascinated.

'Fancy seeing plants growing out here like this,' said Aggie, bending down to get a closer look. 'Never thought there would be such pretty flowers growing in the sand like that.'

'It's amazing they even survive,' agreed Mandy.

They took the opportunity to stretch their legs and have a wander around, marvelling at anything that captured their eye.

Back on the road, they passed more artesian bores and struck some more nasty corrugation on the road. Suddenly there was a cry of alarm from Harvey sitting by the window at the rear of the bus.

'Stop!' he yelled

'Bill brought the bus to an abrupt halt and turned around to see what the problem was. Harvey was up and out of his seat, heading for the door.

'We're about to lose the battery,' he said in alarm.

'Bill opened the door for Harvey to get off and they both went around to the battery compartment situated at the right rear corner of the bus. There, in all its glory was the battery hanging outside the bus, thankfully still strapped to the sliding arm bracket. The door of the battery housing had worked itself loose with all the bouncing on the corrugated roads and had swung open. The latch holding the sliding arm had also worked itself loose allowing the arm to swing out, thankfully with the battery still attached.

Bill rummaged around in his toolbox and after securing the battery back in its housing, set about taping the door closed in the hope that the tape would hold until they got to Birdsville.

'It's okay folks,' said Bill as he climbed back into his seat, nothing major, the battery door has come loose, that's all.'

They headed off once again and as Harvey was sitting directly over the battery housing, he told Bill he would keep an eye on it in case it happened again. The next few kilometres bouncing over the corrugated road proved that the running repairs might just hold.

'There's cattle yards and a stock truck over there,' Gus pointed out. 'Must be a homestead around here somewhere?'

'There is,' said Bill, 'Clifton Hills Homestead.'

'Is it a big station?'

'Yes, last I heard it covered seven million

acres and was carrying around twenty thousand shorthorn cattle. Each of those beasties can sell for around $1100 to $1200 a piece. They reckon it's the second largest cattle station on earth, and it's been under the same ownership since it was established in 1876.

'Perhaps we could stop here for afternoon tea,' responded Tess, glancing at her watch and looking around for trees or cover for people to pee behind.

By now, the skies were clearing and the sun was out but it was still windy. They quickly had their cuppas and snacks then got back on the bus; they were now on the final leg of the day's journey.

They overtook a couple of people on motorbikes loaded with camping gear, prompting Jack to remark that he didn't think he would be adventurous enough to attempt the Birdsville Track on a motorbike. Most of the others agreed.

'I dunno,' said Sam, contemplating, 'might be fun.'

'Be a lot more reliable than that bus over there,' said Lena, pointing out the window.

Bill slowed down as they passed the rusting skeleton of an old yellow double-decker bus set back a short distance from the road.

'Well I never,' said Harvey, 'what on earth is something like that doing way out here?'

'Probably from that movie, *Priscilla Queen of the Desert*,' offered Jan in all seriousness. Nobody knew the real story, so they decided they would settle for that.

As the sun drifted closer to the horizon, Tess became fascinated with the cloud formations and the changing colours of the sky, she took several photos each time the light changed. By the time they pulled up outside the Birdsville Hotel, the sky was bathed in brilliant red and gold.

'Good grief,' what are those things in the trailers over there?' gasped Lena as they drove into Birdsville, 'are they camels?'

She pointed to three large, stock trailers crammed full of camels, eyes peering curiously over the top of the metal sides.

'They sure are,' said Bill, 'they'll be here for the races.

'Races? Surely you don't mean they race those poor things?' Lena was horrified.

'They do,' said Bill, 'and they have horse

racing here too. Big events. People fly in from all over the country, some even come from overseas. Small planes line up along the runway and people sleep out in the open under the wings,' he said. 'Been to one or two race days myself, it's quite an experience.'

'I didn't know they even had camels in Australia?' said Jenny.

'Camels were introduced in 1840, said Bill, flicking through his notebook. 'They were ideal in the early colonisation of the country. Here's something interesting I found,' he said, and began reading: 'In 1839 Lieutenant-Colonel George Gawler decided that camels should be imported to work in the more arid regions of Australia, so they ordered some from the Canary Islands the following year. Sadly, all but one of the camels died en-route, the surviving one they called Harry. He was used for inland exploration by a man called John Horrocks who went looking for new agricultural land in 1846.' Bill did a bit of a chuckle at this point. 'This poor blighter became known as the man who got shot by his own camel. Apparently, he was preparing to take a shot at a bird when Harry the camel, who was kneeling beside him, moved causing the gun to fire injuring Horrocks middle finger of his right hand and a row of teeth. He did survive but the tragic thing was, he died of his wounds three weeks later. When more camels did arrive here safely, they wouldn't work for the white folk so handlers from Afghan had to be recruited to come and work them. Wills and Burke, if you haven't heard of them, Tess and I will fill you in tomorrow, were among the first to use camels when they were surveying this area in 1860.'

Once Bill had answered all the questions about camels, he proceeded to get the suitcases out of the trailer. Tess went into reception, leaving the passengers to disembark by themselves. She was warmly welcomed by the staff who jumped in to help with the suitcases and show the passengers to their rooms. Tess was pleasantly surprised to find brand new beautifully appointed, motel units with white stone floors. She wasn't sure what she was expecting, maybe old wooden hotel rooms perhaps, but certainly nothing like this.

'Are these units all new?' she asked the young man delivering the suitcases.

'Yes, upgrades have been done here and in Marree and Innamincka. Tourism is really picking up around here now,' he said, obviously pleased.

Tess had confirmed dinner for six thirty and breakfast the next morning for six a.m. It would be an early start as they had a long way to go. Bill and Tess had discussed these two big Outback days in-depth the night before. It had been five hundred and nineteen kilometres from Maree to Birdsville and though it would be a hundred kms less from Birdsville to Innamincka, the tracks and the terrain would be rougher and more remote and, most importantly, they needed to be at their destination before nightfall. This next leg of the trip would be the most challenging.

There were a few local people in the bar and restaurant that night, excitement was brewing for the upcoming camel races. Any event in such remote places is a big deal, and this was no exception. One of the passengers enquired about a painting on the wall depicting a woman standing outside a house, surrounded by a dry and empty vastness. It was dark and brooding and the woman was in obvious despair.

In answer to the question, one of the locals explained that it was about a woman whose husband had to go away to find work during a drought. They had to sell off all their stock so he had to source an income elsewhere. He would be gone for weeks at a time, leaving his wife and two young daughters to fend for themselves as best they could between his visits home. On this occasion he had been gone for several weeks and the wife had run out of food. She had no idea when her husband would return, or if he was even still alive. She didn't want to watch her children slowly starving to death so she killed them. Her husband came home a few days later to find her delirious and wailing over their graves out in the back yard, mourning her babies.'

'Is that really true?' asked Jenny, tears in her eyes.

'So they say,' said the storyteller.

Dinner was a lively affair, there was lots of banter and laughter with the locals as the wine and beer flowed. When Tess reminded everyone of their early start in the morning some of them decided they had better have an early night, although a couple of the men opted to stay up and keep chatting with their new 'mates'. Tess and Bill wisely chose to go to bed early, tomorrow they would need to be on their game.

Day 9 – Birdsville to Innamincka
via Cordillo Downs

The group staggered out to breakfast in dribs and drabs from six o'clock the next morning. Tess was pleased to see that they were all in the dining room by six thirty, even those who had stayed on socialising the night before. They enjoyed their hearty cooked breakfasts of baked beans, sausages, scrambled eggs, bacon, tomatoes and hashbrowns swallowed down with orange or apple juice, tea and coffee. Tess stuck to her toast and coffee and watched while Bill tucked into a big plate of everything. He caught her watching him and beamed gleefully.

'Love these cooked breakfasts,' he said.

'Well, make the most of it, you'll probably be back to cereal and toast when you get home,' she laughed.

'You're dead right about that,' he chuckled.

Tess finished her breakfast and stood up. 'See you out at the bus.' She went back to her room to finish packing and pay their account at reception.

Everyone was on the bus, bright eyed, bushy tailed and ready to go by seven thirty.

'Everyone all good?' asked Tess, while Bill filled out his logbook.

'Yes but I still had some red dust in my suitcase when I opened it up last night, can you believe it?' said Lena, a little annoyed.

'Me too,' chorused a couple of others.

'We've got a couple more days of this I'm afraid, so we will just have to put up with it. It's a big day today. We have a slab of water on board, just help yourself to a bottle when you need it. Please stay hydrated, it's very important you do that. Do you have snack bars and fruit with you?'

'Yes,' they affirmed.

'Good. The hotel has prepared us some picnic lunches, the morning tea box is stocked full of biscuits, tea and coffee, and the thermoses are full. Bill has filled the tank to the brim and we have a full jerry can as well so we're ready to go.' She sat back in her seat and looked across at her driver.

'First stop, the Birdsville Working Museum.'

'Yep,' said Bill, 'it's just up the road here.'

The museum proved to be a wonderful depiction of the area's history, the highlight proving to be 'Geraldine', a dear old mule walking in circles turning a wooden wheel that operated a chaff cutter. It was still a bit windy but at least the sun was shining, the skies were clear and the numerous patches of deep red flowers with black centres was enough to brighten anyone's day.

'Sturt Desert Peas,' said Tess as Aggie bent down beside her to take a closer look. 'Aren't they stunning.'

'They are,' breathed Aggie in awe, 'I've never seen anything quite like these before. And they just grow wild here in the desert?'

'They do,' said Tess. 'Unfortunately, we are bit late to see them in all their glory but a few weeks ago we would have seen acres and acres of them along the roadside.'

'That must be truly breath-taking,' enthused Aggie.

Bill put on his headset as they set off from

the museum.

'You may or may not be aware,' he began, 'that we are on the edge of the Simpson Desert here, in the Shire of Diamantina, and for a short time we will be in Queensland before we duck back into South Australia. Our next stop is the Cadelga ruins, about 10kms south of the South Australian border. I will tell you more about that when we get there.'

There was a rustling of paper as a couple of the passengers wrestled with their large Australian maps, trying to shape them into a useable size so they could follow along. Tess hauled out the new Outback map she had just purchased in Birdsville and opened it up to follow the road as well. The back of the large map was covered in valuable information which she had sat up reading the night before. The road wasn't too bad until they turned off the Birdsville Developmental Road onto the Cordillo Downs track, then it got a bit rough and dusty.

'This is pretty much what the road will be like until we get to Innamincka,' advised Bill.

They travelled in silence for a while as they took in their surroundings, 'looking for the difference', as Bill had suggested. Some old ruins came into view and he brought the bus stop on the side of the track just before a river crossing. Trees filled with hundreds of white plumed corellas lined the riverbank. The tree line stretched way off into the distance following the river, while the land on either side of it appeared to be bare and barren.

'Toilet trees to the left and right of us,' informed Bill.' 'Ladies to the left, men to the right.'

'There's toilet paper in a box up the front here, and some wet wipes to wash your hands.'

As they got out of the bus, one or two of the passengers wandered over to take photos of the birds.

As soon as they got close to the trees all hell broke loose. The nervous corellas took to the air in a deafening wave of white chaos. The screeching frightened the life out of everyone. Once the birds had all settled down again, Bill called everyone over to the ruins while Tess set up for morning tea. He began telling them about the old Cadelga Outstation.

'These buildings were made using stone and timber. This area was originally known as Cadelgo Downs, the holding being taken up by a Robert Frew from Cunnamulla in 1877. However, in 1903, this holding was taken over by Cordillo Downs and because of drought and the depression, the station ended up being abandoned somewhere between 1931 and 1936. By 1950 the whole place had fallen into disrepair and sadly that is how it remains today. About ninety kilometres that-a-way,' said Bill pointing further down the road, 'is the famous Cordillo Downs Woolshed, which will be our next stop.'

'Why is the woolshed famous?' asked Harvey.

'You'll see when we get there,' smiled Bill non-committedly.

Bottles of water were passed around, cardigans and sweatshirts were shucked off, the day was warming up. They grabbed a cuppa and wandered around the ruins; a couple of the ladies paddled barefoot in the river. When Bill started up the bus a short time later, they reluctantly climbed back on board.

'Got a lot of ground to cover today folks, unfortunately we won't have too much time to spend at each stop,' Bill explained as they took their time taking their seats.

They covered the next ninety kilometres to Cordillo Downs Woolshed in good time. Bill pulled up at the woolshed gates and turned around in his seat to talk to the passengers.

'Cordillo Downs once covered seven thousand eight hundred square kilometres,' he said, 'it gets around a hundred and sixty-seven mils of rain in a year. This was the largest sheep station in Australia and in the 1880's Cordillo set a record of shearing over eighty-five thousand sheep in one season, in this woolshed. It's a heritage-listed building now. As you can see, it is made of stone with a curved tin roof, that's because there was a lack of timber in the area. When you look at the compound around the homestead you will see most of the rooves are rounded.'

'It's certainly an impressive set-up,' said Gus. 'won't find anything like this back home.'

'It's pointless comparing anything in Australia to what we have back home,' said Mandy, 'I mean look at the difference in the size of the two countries for starters.' Gus shrugged and fell silent as Bill continued reading from his notebook.

'The run was first taken up by John Frazer from Victoria in 1875, back then it was known as Cardilla. He let the property go in 1878 and a ballot was held with the lease going to Edgar Chapman. He in turn sold it to Peter Waite of the Beltana Pastoral Company in 1883. The property was stocked with just over ten thousand sheep, nearly six hundred cattle and about thirty horses. In 1903 the property was amalgamated with two other stations, Cadelga and Haddon Downs, and had a flock of sheep of around eighty-five thousand by 1905. Beltana owned the property until 1981, although the homestead was abandoned for a few years during the 1930s. It was then sold to the Brook family under the name Brookman Holdings, for $1.2 million. Apparently old Bill Brook was eighty-one years old when he brought the property. Turns out he had been employed here as a ringer in 1918 for thirty shillings a week. As far as I can tell, the Brook family still own the property.'

The group meandered around looking at the various pieces of equipment on display before Bill shepherded everyone back to the bus. He flipped through his notebook.

'Here's something else you might find interesting,' he said, as the passengers came back through the gate. 'Mail was delivered out here by air from about 1949. In fact, the mail was delivered by air to quite a large area which included Mungerannie, Clifton Hills and Glengyle,'

'Hang on,' said Doug, 'Wait till I get my map so we can see where you're talking about.'

Doug got his well-worn map from inside the bus and spread it out against the sloped side of the trailer.

'Let's have a look,' said Bill leaning in to get a closer look at the names on the map. 'So, this area here, plus Davenport Downs, Morney Plains, Mount Leonard, Durrie, Mulks, Tanbar, Durham Downs, Nappa Merrie, Lake Pure and Naryilco,' he said as he circled his finger in a wide arc over the map.

'That's quite a mail run,' whistled Gus tilting his hat back and scratching his head. 'No wonder they had to do it by air.'

'A couple of other notes I have here,' continued Bill, 'Cooper Creek,' he pointed it out on the map, 'broke its banks in 1950 causing widespread flooding right through here.'

'Hard to imagine that,' considered Frank gazing around at their vast dry surroundings.

'And they reckon a meteor landed somewhere on this property in 1954. The bright flash and ball of fire was also seen in Innamincka.' They mulled over the map for a while before Bill suggested they get packed up and back on the road.

Everyone was quiet as they settled down for the next part of their bumpy dusty ride through Cordillo Downs. When Tess spotted a row of trees in the distance ahead, she suggested to Bill it might be a good place to stop for lunch. He agreed. Tess was surprised at how much water there was in the small creek, while the rest of the area seemed so dry. Bill set up the fold out table while Tess hauled out the box of sandwiches and cake from the back of the bus.

'Damn,' she said, then laughed. 'Not so much sandwiches today as dustwiches,' she grinned up at Bill. 'Good thing they are well wrapped, I guess the kitchen staff at Birdsville knew what they were doing.' Turning to the group she said, 'Come and grab something to eat. Sorry you are going to have to blow the dust off the wrappings first, but that's life in the outback.'

They stood around in groups, sat under a tree or paddled in the creek as they ate and drank their water or fruit drinks. Some put a piece of cake or fruit away for later, others tucked in heartily and ate whatever was on offer. Nobody seemed too bothered about tea and coffee so they decided to leave that until later down the track. June suggested they have a group photo taken in front of a tree with red dirt and blue sky as the backdrop. Bill topped up the fuel tank with the spare gas in the jerry-can and they were off again.

'You know I've just realised, we haven't seen any traffic since we left Birdsville,' said Jack.

'No, we haven't have we?' pondered Sam. 'Bit scary if you break down out here and there's no one around, especially as there's no phone reception or anything.'

'That's why you should always carry an EPIRB or a satellite phone and plenty of water when you travel in the outback,' said Bill.

They were still on the Cordillo Downs property but would be turning off towards Innamincka within an hour or so. In total they would be driving across the property, including stops, for six hours.

When they approached the Wills and Burke dig tree turn off Tess asked, 'Have we got enough daylight hours to go out to the memorial and the tree?'

Bill pulled up and the two of them poured over the mud map.

'We've enough water, fuel and daylight if we take that loop there, which will get us back on to the track further up, provided we don't take too long at the dig tree site,' said Bill, tracing his finger along a loop road.

'Okay,' Tess decided, 'let's go and have a look at the dig tree, it would be a shame to come all this way and not see it.' She turned to her passengers who were waiting patiently for an explanation for the stop. 'Bill and I have decided that we have enough fuel and daylight to take a quick detour to see the Burke and Wills dig tree.'

'See the what?' asked Leana.

'The Burke and Wills dig tree,' said Tess. 'Have any of you heard about Burke and Wills?'

There was a tentative nod of the head from a couple of the group but generally she got blank looks. As Bill turned off on the loop road he handed Tess his headset, she placed it on her head and, glancing down at the notes she had foraged from her briefcase, began to tell the story.

'Burke and Wills were part of a nineteen-man expedition which began in 1860 with the intention of crossing Australia from Melbourne right up through the middle of the country to the Gulf of Carpentaria.' She could hear a rustle of paper as the maps came out.

'Whew, that's a mighty long way to go on foot or by horse,' said Sam.

'Yes it was,' replied Tess, 'three thousand, two hundred and fifty kilometres to be exact.'

'How long did it take them?' Sam again.

'Just sit back and listen,' offered Bill, 'give Tess a chance to tell the story, which will no doubt answer most of your questions.'

'Sorry,' said Sam, 'carry on Tess.'

Tess smiled at him.

'I like that you are interested Sam, it is one of my favourite stories from Australian history and I love sharing it. Anyhoo, moving right along,' she laughed, 'the expedition left Melbourne at four o'clock on the afternoon of the 20th of August 1860. They took with them twenty tonnes of equipment, including enough food to last two years, a cedar-topped oak camp table with two chairs, rockets, flags and a Chinese gong. All this was loaded on to six wagons. It was winter and slow going at first because of bad weather, poor roads and the horse wagons kept breaking down. They had twenty-six camels, most of them had only just arrived in the country from India, twenty-three horses and six wagons. Of the nineteen men in the expedition party there were six Irishmen, five Englishmen, four camel drivers, three of them Afghan the other one Indian, plus three Germans and an American.' Tess looked up from her notes and glanced back at the group. 'Quite a mixed bag of nationalities wouldn't you say,' she said.

'Sure was,' they laughed. 'How did they all get along?' Sam asked.

'Probably as well as any mixed group under the circumstances. As you can imagine, they went through some pretty tough times out there in the wilderness, enough to test the strength of the strongest of men.' She picked up her notes and continued.

'The expedition reached Swan Hill on the 6th of September and arrived in Balranald on the

15$^{th\ of}$ September.' More rustling of maps. 'It was here that they decided to lighten the load and they left behind their sugar, lime juice and some of their guns and ammunition. When they got to Gambala on the 24th of September, the expedition leader, Robert O'Hara Burke, decided to load some of the provisions onto the camels for the first time, and he ordered the men to walk, to ease the burden on the horses. Their luggage was also restricted to fourteen kilograms. Now here's the part that answers your question about how they got along,' Tess turned and smiled at Sam. 'When they got to Bilbarka on the Darling River, Burke and his second-in-command, Landells, argued after Burke opted to dump sixty gallons of rum that Landells had brought along to feed the camels, believing that it prevented scurvy.'

'Hah, that's a likely story,' scoffed Gus, bet he was a sly drinker.' They all laughed.

Tess continued. 'When they reached Kinchega, Landells resigned, followed by the expedition's surgeon Dr Hermann Beckler. This is where the third-in-command, William John Wills became second-in-command. It took them two months to travel seven hundred and fifty kilometres from Melbourne to Menindee, they arrived there on the 12th of October. Apparently, the regular mail coach could do it in little more than a week.' Everyone laughed again. 'By the time they got to Menindee, five officers had resigned, thirteen members of the expedition had been fired and eight new men had been hired. At the time this expedition was going on, there was another experienced explorer, John McDougall Stuart who was also attempting an inland crossing of the continent from south to north. A reward of £2000 had been offered by the South Australian Government so they were both vying for it. Burke was worried that Stuart might beat him to the north coast as they were making such slow progress, about two miles a day, so he decided to split the group. He took the strongest horses, seven of the fittest men and a small amount of equipment. He planned to push on to Cooper Creek and wait for the others to catch up. He arrived

at Cooper on the 11th of November and formed a depot and camp, but a plague of rats forced them to form a second depot further downstream at Bullah Bullah Waterhole. They named this place Fort Wills. It was expected that Burke would wait until March the following year before continuing to push north rather than continue on in the hot Australian Summer. However, he only waited until

the 16th of December before deciding to make a dash for the Gulf of Carpentaria. He left William Brahe, his third-in-command, and three of the men in charge of the depot with orders to wait for three months for their return. The rest, Wills, John King, and Charles Gray would accompany Burke. They took six camels, one horse and enough food for just three months. Wills was a little more conservative and after reviewing the maps and taking a more realistic view of the task ahead, he secretly instructed Brahe to wait for four months.'

It was at this point that they reached the site of the Burke and Wills dig tree. Bill pulled up and opened the door, letting the engine idle for a few moments before shutting it down.

'Oh look,' exclaimed Aggie excitedly, 'there's a Pelican. I've always wanted to see one up close.'

'Well, it's your lucky day then,' smiled Tess. 'Have you got your camera ready?'

'Sure have,' laughed Aggie, loaded up and ready to go.'

'Okay everyone, let's get out and I will tell

you what happened to Burke and Wills while we are standing underneath the tree,' said Tess. When they had all run their fingers over, and taken photos of, the markings on the tree, and the Pelican, Tess picked up the story.

'Don't forget this is mid-summer when they decided to do this push to the north, the temperatures sometimes reached fifty degrees in the shade.'

'Whew,' exclaimed Doug, 'that's pretty damn hot.'

Tess nodded. 'Despite the heat, travelling was relatively easy. There had been some recent rain so water could still be found, and the Aborigines they came across were peaceful, contrary to what they expected.' Mindful of the time and waning daylight, Tess wrapped up the tale.

'Long story short, they couldn't reach their destination because of mangrove swamps. It had taken them fifty-nine days to get there and there was only twenty-seven days of food left so they needed to get back to Cooper Creek. On the way back they shot and ate three camels and they also had to shoot their horse, Billy. They ate a plant called portulaca to extend their food supply and caught and ate a black headed python which gave then dysentery. It was now March the 25th and they were just south of what is now Boulia. Gray was caught stealing food. Burke beat the living daylights out of him and eventually the poor man couldn't walk. He died of dysentery on the 8th of April. They finally reached the Cooper Camp, here,' Tess waved her hand around, 'on the 21st of April only to find the camp had been abandoned just hours earlier.'

'Oh, that is so tragic,' said Mona sadly.

'Yes, and what was worse is that these poor, tired, starving men missed the scratchings on this tree indicating that there was food buried beneath it. But let's get back on the bus, I will tell you the rest as we go, it's getting late.' She wandered over to Bill who was crouched down beside the trailer wheel. 'Something wrong?' she asked.

Bill looked up at her, frowning. 'The damn bearings have become so hot they've welded themselves to the shaft. The wheel is still spinning but I don't know how long it will stay on for.'

'Oh,' said Tess, not sure what more to say.

'Come on,' said Bill. 'We'd best get going, we'll be running out of daylight before we get there at this rate. I will just keep an eye on it and if it falls off, we can stow the suitcases on the back seats of the bus and leave the trailer behind.'

Tess and Bill opted not to inform the passengers about the trailer wheel, no need to cause them any concern. Once they got underway Tess finished her Burke and Wills story.

'Just to wrap up the story folks, Burke and Wills died around the end of June 1861. Several relief expeditions were sent out to find them. Altogether seven men died and only one man, the Irish soldier John King, crossed the continent with the expedition and returned alive to Melbourne.'

'Damn and blast.' The expletives from Bill caught Tess by surprise.

'The trailer wheel?' she whispered.

'No, look,' he pointed ahead. He got out of the bus and walked up to a gate and tried to open it. He returned stony faced and climbed back in the bus. 'Bloody thing is padlocked,' he hissed.

'What do we do now?' asked Tess, can we go around it?'

'Nope, only thing we can do is go back the way we came,' he said ruefully.

'But that...'

'I know,' said Bill rolling his eyes. 'They've locked the gate on us,' he told the passengers after he'd donned his headset, 'so it looks like we will have to go back the way we came. Not to worry, these things happen,' he attempted a reassuring smile as he looked at them in is rear view mirror. He was grateful that it hadn't sunk in with them that they were now in a bit of a perilous situation. The light was fading and the fuel gauge was showing less than what he was comfortable with. The passengers grew silent as they sensed the tension in the two people sitting at the front of the bus. The two people they were relying on to keep them safe and get them home.

As they drove back past Cooper Creek again,

June asked about the trees lining the waterway.

'Northern river red gums and coolibahs,' answered Bill. He glanced across the creek. 'That dark spindly stuff growing underneath the trees is called Lignum, it's one of the few plants that thrives in the desert and at certain times of the year they will have yellow or white flowers.'

Silence fell again as they drove quietly all the way back out to where they had turned off more than an hour earlier. They turned east and headed towards Innamincka; they still had another fifty kilometres of slow driving on a rough dirt track before they got to their overnight accommodation. Bill kept glancing in his side mirror watching for sparks or smoke coming from the trailer wheel, or worse, seeing it fall off altogether. Eventually the group started chatting again and all was going well until there was a loud bang under the bus. Tess's heart thudded in her chest.

'What was that?'

'Blown tyre by the sounds of it,' mumbled Bill as he got out of the bus. When he came back, he confirmed his suspicions. One of the inner dual wheels on the back has blown,' he said to the passengers. 'But it's okay, we still have five others,' he tried a smile. 'You might hear a bit of flapping going on under the bus but don't worry it's only the loose bits of tyre.'

With that he turned back in his seat, put the bus in gear and carried on up the rough dirt track.

Tess noted how strained he looked. It didn't help that the passengers had once again fallen deathly quiet.

'Hand me the headset,' she said to Bill.

He handed it over, she put it on and began singing. 'You are my sunshine, my only sunshine...,' she was relieved when they all started joining in. When one song finished someone would start another one and so it went on. Then, without any fanfare, the skies went dark, very very dark.

'It's like the inside of a bloody cow,' remarked Gus.

'You can say that again,' said Frank. 'Hope Bill can see where he's going.'

'We're following tyre tracks,' said Tess, 'so long as they lead us to Innamincka we will be okay,' she turned to try and assure them with a smile. 'Come on, what's another song.' They started singing again, the sing along songs turning into hymns.

'Rather appropriate,' thought Tess, 'we could do with some Angels on our shoulders right now.' She glanced across at Bill as he threw a rag across the dashboard.

'What's the matter?'

'I don't want to look at the fuel gauge right now,' he said quietly.

'Oh,' said Tess, becoming more alarmed. She considered their situation. It was pitch black; all they could see were tyre marks on a rough dirt track in the beams of the headlights. They were running low on fuel now because of the detour they had to take, and then there were the added complications of the trailer wheel threatening to part company with the trailer at any moment, and the flapping of the shredded tyre which didn't do anything to calm anyone's nerves. What if another tyre was to blow out, what if they ran out of diesel? Would anyone know where to find them? They didn't have an EPIRB with them but they did at least have the satellite phone.

Tess started singing again and the group joined her, this time with more gusto and within a very short time they were singing hymns.

It seemed like an eternity before they spotted the lights of Innamincka. They were now more than two hours behind schedule, and they assumed there would be some worried people waiting for them. She wasn't wrong. As they pulled up outside the hotel they were still singing hymns as one of the staff came running out to greet them.

'Thank God you are here, we were getting worried,' she said.

'So were we,' said Tess, 'but we made it with the help of these guys singing hymns, and I'm sure we had a bus full of Angels with us as well.'

She turned and smiled at the relief on the faces of her passengers. Survivors' euphoria would begin to set in before long, they all knew the last leg of their journey could easily have gone 'tits up' but thank God it hadn't. They had arrived safe and sound and, to Bill's relief, the trailer was still intact.

The staff member ushered them inside while a couple of others came out to help Bill unload the trailer. Tess followed the group inside and wondered why some of them were cheering. She glanced up at the television screen on the wall to see that the New Zealand All Blacks were beating the Aussies ten to nil. The two Aussie blokes sitting underneath the television trying to have a quiet beer were not impressed with these bloody Kiwi's applauding their embarrassing loss.

Dinner was a lively affair with drinks flowing freely as the relief and euphoria enveloped everyone. But, by the time they'd eaten their meals and had a couple of drinks, they were ready for their beds.

It had been an exceptionally long day, and despite the odds they were still alive and well. They were all suddenly very tired. Tomorrow was another day, hopefully not as adventurous as this one had been.

Day 10 – Innamincka to Tibooburra

Some of the group were tucking into their hearty cooked breakfasts, revived and ready to face another day, when Tess finally appeared. She was feeling tired and worn out this morning but she wasn't the last one to turn up for breakfast for a change. Bill was nowhere to be seen either.

'Morning everyone, how are you all this morning?'

'Good thanks Tess,' they chorused.

'Looking forward to another adventurous day,' said Lena.

'Hopefully not one as adventurous as yesterday,' sighed Tess.

'Here, come and sit down and I'll get you some coffee,' offered Aggie, you look tired this morning.'

'Thank you Aggie, yes I am pretty pooped I have to admit. Has anyone seen Bill this morning?'

'Gone to fill up the bus and get the blown tyre replaced,' offered Gus.

When Tess had finished packing, she wheeled her bag out to the bus and went to talk with Bill as he was loading the trailer.

'How did you get on with the tyre?'

'All fixed thank goodness, not sure about the trailer though. They couldn't do much about it here so I'll just have to take a chance that it will get us to Tibooburra, hopefully there's someone there who can fix it.' He checked to make sure no-one could overhear then said quietly, 'You know how I was worried about the fuel gauge last night?' Tess nodded. 'It's a three hundred litre tank, damn thing took 303 litres this morning, we must have been running on fumes.'

'And hymns and prayers,' Tess said thoughtfully. 'Let's hope there's no dramas today. How are you feeling, I guess you must be pretty tired too, it was a hugely stressful day for you.'

'It was, and yes, I am a bit tired, but I had a good sleep and another big, cooked breakfast. Everyone ready to go?' he asked as he stacked the last plastic wrapped suitcase in the trailer.

'I'll go and check. I haven't paid the account yet.'

'I take it you want to have a look around before we push on for Tibooburra?' Bill asked Tess as she settled herself in her seta. 'By my reckoning we have around 300kms to go today but it will take us more than eight hours. Keep in mind that it will be rough dirt track and corrugations most of the way. It's up to you.'

Tess pondered for a moment. 'It's just gone eight thirty, we will have to stop for lunch and morning tea along the way which will add another hour. Maybe just a quick drive around before we leave then, what do you think?'

'I agree, we don't know what's going to happen with that trailer, so we need to have a little time up our sleeves and perhaps shorten the breaks a bit. At least we will be driving into civilisation by the time it gets dark, if we are held up along the way.'

Tess nodded and as they drove around the settlement, she read through the information she'd picked up at reception then, as they left Innamincka, she donned Bill's headset and began talking.

'This area was popular back in the late 1800's early 1900's for drovers driving their stock along Cooper Creek. Apparently, Sir Sidney Kidman was one of them.'

'That's Nicole Kidman's family isn't it?' enquired Mandy.

'I believe so,' said Tess turning back to continue reading from her leaflet.

White settlement in the area saw the establishment of the Innamincka Station in 1872. Ten years later, a police outpost was set up followed by a general store two years later and the pub a year after that.

The town was actually proclaimed as 'Hopetoun' in 1890 after the Governor of Victoria.

However, it was officially changed to Innamincka in 1892 after intense opposition to the proclaimed name.

The town continued to flourish and at one time included a blacksmith, school, hotel, police station, saddler and a few small houses. Until Federation in 1901, Innamincka prospered as a customs depot where state taxes were collected from increasing numbers of drovers who moved cattle from Queensland into South Australia and down the Strzelecki. An Inland Mission Hospital/Nursing Home and Flying Doctor Base was established in 1929, but eventually, all facilities closed, and the town was abandoned in 1952.

'One of the bar staff told me there was a huge pile of old beer bottles here when the town closed down,' said Gus. 'There was not enough patronage to have kegs back then, so all the beer was sold in bottles. He said there was a flood in 1956 which washed what was left of the hotel, the police station, half the Flying Doctors' base and all the old bottles downstream. Must have been quite a sight.'

This started a sharing of information and observations amongst the group, so Tess left them to it. Bill interrupted at one point to let them know they had just crossed the border briefly into Queensland, and to watch for the sign that said they were about to cross from there into New South Wales. The road was no longer the softer red dirt, or bulldust, it was white, hard-packed corrugation, and most uncomfortable. It was along this bumpy road that the curtain on Bill's window decided to slide off the rail and fall at his feet. He left it there.

After they had been on the road for some time, they came up over the brow of a hill and there before them stood several tall chimney stacks spewing orange flames into a clear blue sky, looking distinctly out of place in the desert.

'Good grief, what on earth is that?' Lena

gasped.

'Gas fields,' explained Bill. 'That will be the Moomba Camp over there. It began operating about four years ago, in 2004. As you can see there are six wells plus the infrastructure required to operate it. They anticipate it will supply eight percent of the gas requirements for South Australia.'

They could see a large compound with accommodation units and lots of satellite dishes.

'They must be able to get good TV reception with all those satellite dishes,' Harvey chimed in.'

'And watch the footy,' smiled Jack.

'Oh, you and your damned footy Jack,' Sam grumbled as she punched Jack on the arm.

They were back on the Strzelecki Track again now and were surprised and delighted to see emu's and a lot more wildflowers along the way, mainly yellow, white and purple ones.

The change in terrain took them over the roller coaster sand dunes again but at least it broke the monotony of the long straight roads that endlessly disappeared into the distance, and the roads here were not so corrugated now. They began to encounter traffic in the form of road trains, with two or more trailers on behind. The first time it happened, Bill spotted the tell-tale dust cloud in the distance, pulled over to the side of the road at a suitable spot, turned the engine off, shut down the air conditioning and made sure all the windows were shut tight.

'What's happening?' asked Lena.

'You'll see in a minute,' was Bill's response.

As they sat in silence one of the passengers spotted the dust cloud ahead and could see the truck.

'It's a road train,' said Gus excitedly.

The passengers were in awe as the truck

rumbled past, just as they were the first time they had seen one on the way to Birdsville. The truck driver gave Bill a friendly wave as he went past. It took a minute or two for the trailing dust cloud to dissipate before Bill started up the bus, switched on the air conditioning and pulled back out onto the road. They would do that three more times on this leg of their journey.

'They'll be going to the gas fields I suppose?' asked Gus.

'Yep,' confirmed Bill, 'their supplies come in by road. Some of it will go on further to Innamincka too of course.'

They reached Merty Merty Station and decided to stop for lunch.

'This station was set up in 1919,' said Bill, glancing at his notes. Sidney Kidman bought the property in 1924 but he only ran stock on it. There is an old homestead beside the Strzelecki Creek and the Strzelecki Track passes right through this property.

'Not many places to pee in private around these parts,' said Bill, looking around as he got out of the bus. 'There's a tree over there. I've got a bit of canvas in the boot; you could hold that up as a screen for each other if you like.'

The idea brought forth a few giggles, but everyone took it in their stride and made the most of the opportunity to water the desert while they had the chance.

They enjoyed wandering around eating

their lunch and stooping now and again to get a closer look at the wildflowers or some other living thing defying the odds.

'What are these plants Tess?' asked June.

'I have no idea, let me have a look in my little book.' She hooked a small booklet out of her briefcase and started flicking through the pages. With heads together pouring through the coloured photographs of plants and flowers, they came to the conclusion that it was sandhill Wattle. 'We might see some whitewood and narrow leaf Hop-bush too,' said Tess glancing around.

'And Cane-grass,' added June. She now had Tess's book clutched firmly in her hands.

The ladies became interested at that point and after glancing at the photos, set about searching for said plants.

'Better keep moving folks,' said Bill, after a few minutes 'we've still got a lot of ground to cover.

Reluctantly the ladies returned to the bus, with one or two gently carrying a piece of a plant or a flower to show the others.

Bill did a quick inspection of the bus and trailer before climbing into his seat, so far so good. They trundled up and over more sand dunes, some of them as high as 15 metres, and they trundled down long straight roads through an ever-changing landscape of trees, shrubs and red dirt desert with the occasional animal or emu making an appearance along the way. Eventually they reached the Cameron Corner Store.

'We'll stop here for a cuppa and a toilet break,' said Tess. 'If you want anything else, including cold drinks, there will be some available in the shop. Our next stop is Cameron Corner itself; I will tell you all about that when we get there.'

Tess wandered off around the compound with her cameras and a cold drink. She enjoyed a bit of time to herself now and then, just to gather her thoughts. She was pleased she had her camera with her when she came across a sign painted on a drum which read:

> G'Day, welcome to Cameron Corner.
> It's not the middle of nowhere,
> it's the centre of everywhere.

She took a photo and moved off towards the sound of laughter coming from the Store. Inside, her passengers were being regaled with stories by the patrons and one or two travellers also passing through the area. She noticed that one or two of her male passengers were clutching mugs of beer.

'Hope you're not leading these people astray,' said Tess as she walked in.

'It's the other way around I reckon,' said the young man behind the bar. 'Haven't had too many Kiwis through these parts, a few grey nomads now and again but certainly not bus groups of Seniors. Bloody hard cases you lot are.' He laughed heartily and everyone else joined in.

Tess smiled to herself and walked outside again planning to pack up the afternoon tea table. To her surprise Bill had already done the deed and was now filling up at the fuel pump. He glanced at his watch.

'Are you concerned about the time Bill?' Tess was beginning to get a bit worried.

'No, not at all, I just don't want to leave anything to chance that's all.' He looked around to make sure they were alone. 'In all my years of driving I never experienced a day like yesterday,' he said quietly. 'It shook me up a bit.'

'I had no idea it bothered you so much Bill. Look, even if we had run out of fuel, we had the SAT phone.'

'I checked the SAT phone this morning and the damn thing's not working, he said looking concerned. Don't know what's wrong with it, phone technology is a bit beyond me,' he confessed.

'What's the worst that can happen between here and Tibooburra?' asked Tess, trying to push down her rising concerns.

'If we do run into any problems there is more traffic coming and going through here so that's a positive at least. Look Tess I'm not anticipating any problems, it's just that I got a little unnerved yesterday watching the fuel gauge hitting empty, waiting for the trailer wheel to come off and listening to the tyre flapping itself to bits under the bus. All the while I kept praying we were following the right tracks in the dark.' He hung up the pump nozzle, placed the cap back on the fuel tank, took a deep breath and turned to look Tess in the eye.

'Sorry Tess, I guess I just needed to offload.

'It's me who should be apologising Bill. Yesterday freaked the shit out of me too. I had nightmares last night, but I never thought you would be feeling this unsettled too. I guess I just assumed that being an experienced driver you would be taking it all in your stride.'

'Normally, if I was on my own I would, but being responsible for the wellbeing and safety of a bus load of people adds a lot of pressure, I'm sure you can relate to that.'

'I can,' sighed Tess. Look, we are in this together, I'm just as responsible for these people as you are, so please don't hesitate to talk to me – about anything. I know how much it helps to off-load at the end of a trying day.'

'Thanks,' he said gruffly. 'Better get this show on the road then, places to go, people to see and all that.' Tess smiled and, stowing her camera on her seat, walked back to the store to prise her travellers away from the bar.

'Come on you lot, we've got a date with the centre of the universe,' she laughed.

'Centre of the universe?' queried Gus, downing the last of his beer.

'Well, the locals sure think it is,' Tess smiled at the barman who raised a glass in agreement.

They drove the short distance to the much photographed dry, tortured tree depicting the intersection between three states of Australia. Once everyone was out of the bus Tess guided them over to the information kiosk and said, 'This is the point where the states of Queensland, New South Wales and South Australia meet.'

'That's why the bloke in the Store said they had a Queensland post code, a New South Wales postal address and a South Australian telephone number,' said Gus, I didn't understand what he meant, now it makes sense. Must be confusing.'

'Each state is in a different time zone, so people love to come here to celebrate New Year three times in the one night,' laughed Tess.

They moved on over to a white stone marker depiction the 'Corner'.

'This fence over here is also quite famous,' continued Tess, 'it's the 'dingo Fence.''

'I've heard of that,' said Gus, 'read about it somewhere.'

Tess opened the notebook she held in her hand and flicked through it. 'The dingo fence was originally a rabbit proof fence built back in the 1880's but it wasn't very successful and fell into disrepair. It was later adapted in 1914 when it was rebuilt to stop dingoes from going from central Australia into south-east Australia and killing the livestock there. It goes from the Great Australian Bight to south-east Queensland through five deserts. And right here where we are standing, is about half- way along that fence. Boundary riders ride up and down the fence to keep it maintained. The fence was originally eight thousand six hundred and fourteen kilometres long but has since been reduced to five thousand six hundred and fourteen kilometres and is now called the Wild Dog Barrier Fence. If you are interested to know more about it you are welcome to read my notes, but for now we'd best keep moving.'

Gus asked if he could read Tess's notes and she handed him her notebook. After he had finished reading about the dog fence, he flicked through the rest of the notebook. Handing it back he asked if she would tell them about the States of Australia, and the Deserts. 'I saw your notes there and they look quite interesting,' he smiled cheekily at her.

Tess took the notebook and flicked it open to the appropriate pages. 'Okay,' she said, 'you asked for it. Here begins our Geography lesson for today.' Everyone laughed. 'How many States are there in Australia?' she asked the group.

'Five,' declared Frank.

'How many think there are five?' she turned in her seat and saw a couple of hands go up.

'So, if you don't think there are five, how many do you think there are?' she asked again.

'I believe there are six,' answered Aggie.

'Correct, so what are they?' asked Tess with a cheeky smile.

One by one they named the States: Northern Territory, Western Australia, Queensland, South Australia, New South Wales, and here they drew a blank.

'What's the sixth one then?' Gus turned around to Aggie.

'Victoria,' she smiled gleefully.

'Oh of course,' the others groaned.

'Now, let's turn to the deserts. How many of those are there in Australia and what are their names?' Tess was pleased to see everyone engaged and interested.

There was a rustling of paper as a couple

of them got out their maps and unfolded them as best they could in the confined space between their seats.

'Strzelecki,' called Gus, obviously pleased with himself.

'Great Victorian Desert,' called Aggie. That's in the Southwest of South Australia and if I am right, I believe it might be the biggest.'

'You are right Aggie, well done, go to the top of the class.' Tess was chuckling along with the rest of them now; they were enjoying themselves.

'Sturt Stony Desert,' called Gus as he found another one on his map. So how many are there then?

'Ten,' said Tess. 'If you can guess them all, I will shout drinks at dinner tonight.' She sat back and marked off the names of the desserts as her passengers discovered them on their maps, some of them crouched down in the aisle beside someone who had a map.

'Simpson.'

'The Great Sandy Desert.'

'Oh look, there's a little Sandy Desert too.'

'Gibson Desert.'

'That's seven,' said Tess encouragingly. 'Just three more.'

The passengers pondered over their maps, swapping them around to share the different versions they had.

'Ah, here's one,' called June, 'Tanami, not sure if I've pronounced if correctly.'

'What about Pilbara?'

'That's not a desert,' came a discouraging reply.

'Arnhem Land looks pretty dry on the map.'

'Still not a desert,' said Tess. 'You need to be back down in South Australia to find Tirari. It's not on my big map but it is on my Outback one if any of you have one of those.'

'I do,' said Aggie, she was enjoying this. 'Ah yes, there it is, Tirari Desert,' she declared.

'I'm impressed,' said Bill, 'damned if I can find anything on those maps.'

'Painted Desert.'

'Well, it's not on the list of the top ten because it's not part of the Great Australian Desert,' said Tess, but fair enough, I will give you that one because I didn't particularly stipulate that they had to be part of the Great Australian Desert. Apparently, it is called the 'painted' desert because of its variety of colours. I haven't seen it yet, but it's on my bucket list.

'You're a bit young to have a bucket list aren't you?' asked Gus. 'Thought that sort of thing was for oldies who thought they were running out of time,' he laughed.

'Never too young to have a bucket list,' responded Tess.

'So how many things have you crossed off the list so far?'

'Ummm, none,' laughed Tess, 'perhaps I should rename it my 'to do' list. Now, as for the last one, Pedirka, it is up around the Witjira National Park I think. I couldn't find it either but there is a track through there called the Pedirka Track. Seeing as we've added in the Painted Desert,' Tess paused, did a quick count and looked at the group, 'the drinks are on me at dinner tonight.'

There was a round of applause after which several conversations started up and Tess sat back in her seat with a smile on her face.'

'Tell you what I've seen other operators do on long days like this,' said Bill, 'they ask questions about what they have seen on the trip since they started. You will be amazed at how much they don't remember straight off. Probably because there's so much to take in.'

'That's a good idea, I'll keep it in mind, thanks Bill.'

As the entered the Sturt National Park area, they noticed speed cameras on poles.

'Never thought you'd see speed cameras on a desert road,' laughed Harvey.

'We're in New South Wales, they have their rules,' explained Bill.

'Kangaroo on the left,' called Gus. Everyone turned to see as it sat there watching them go by. They were still driving on red dirt roads but they were becoming more corrugated the closer they got to Tibooburra. Suddenly the heavy old style television set fell out of its bracket above Tess and Bill's head and crashed down on Bill's left arm. He let out an almighty yelp and quickly the pulled the bus to a stop. Tess was stunned. She looked down at the TV lying on the floor then back up to Bill who was clutching at his arm in obvious pain. Gathering her wits about her, she reached back behind her seat for the first aid kit and pulled out an ice pack and snapped it so that the contents would form a cold compress. She gently applied it to Bill's arm.

'Are you going to be able to drive?' she asked, her mind racing through the possibility of her having to drive the rest of the way.

Bill was taking deep breaths. 'Just give me a minute,' he said wiggling his fingers. 'Don't think anything's broken. Tess dived back into the first aid kit and took out a packet of Panadol tablets. She popped out two and handed them to Bill with a bottle of water. He downed the pills gratefully and sat back in his seat with his head resting on the headrest. Tess turned to the passengers.

'Perhaps you'd like to get some fresh air and stretch your legs for a few minutes while Bill recovers,' she suggested. They all agreed and got out of the bus, huddling together to discuss the situation amongst themselves. They felt for Bill, his arm must be pretty painful.

'I could drive if I have to,' offered Tess, 'I've got my passenger licence, I've just never driven anything bigger than a seventeen-seater van.'

'It's okay Tess, the pain is easing a bit, I think I'll be okay, we don't have all that far to go.' Tess nodded, relieved.

After about twenty minutes the painkillers had kicked in. Bill walked around for a while flexing his arm muscles to keep the blood flowing and eventually decided he should be good to go so they all piled back on the bus. In order to take their minds off Bill's plight Tess suggested they take turns telling their life stories. Doug and Jenny were sitting in the front seat so Doug donned Bill's headset as best he could and started his story.

'I grew up in Matamata, had one sibling, my brother Reggie, short for Reginald. Everyone called him Vege and my name was always spelt as Dug because our surname was Garden.' He waited for the penny to drop and the ensuing chuckling to subside. 'Mum and Dad had a hardware store, but I don't think they made a lot of money. Panic buying was when we sold two of the same item in one day. Stock market crash was when something fell off the shelf, a good day was when Dad sold something, a bad day was when they brought it back. Reggie and I tried to help out as best we could. We would pinch the apples off the neighbour's tree and sell them to the local greengrocer, and we would nick the glass coke bottles from the back of the dairy and sell them back to the dairy owner. In those days we got a halfpenny for every bottle. We did alright too,' he said proudly, and Mum and Dad never knew.'

'Sorry to burst your bubble Doug,' said Jenny with a chuckle, 'but your poor long-suffering parents knew full well what you little toerags got up to. She told me one day when you and I first started courting.'

'Really?' Doug was flabbergasted. 'How did they find out?'

'Well, according to your mother, everyone knew what you and Reggie used to get up to. You weren't considered bad boys, just naughty and mischievous,' she was chuckling. 'Your Mum told me that the shop owners would come and visit them now and then and tell them what you boys had been up to. Apparently, your Mum was embarrassed and offered to pay them back but the shop owners refused and said it was fun watching you boys trying to be little entrepreneurs, not realising everyone knew what you were up to right from the start.'

By now, everyone was roaring with laughter. Doug was embarrassed and a little humiliated at first but ended up laughing along with everyone else. He took the headset off and handed it to Jenny. 'Your turn,' he said smugly.

'No, I would rather hear from someone else,' smiled Jenny as she vacated her front seat and held the headset out to Sam sitting in the seat behind her.'

Sam shrugged and moved forward into the front seat, donning the headset as she settled herself in. 'I come from a family of nine kids, I was the second eldest. We grew up on a sheep farm in the King Country. We weren't what you would call well-off, but there was always food on the table and clothes on our backs, even if they were hand-me-downs most of the time. We used to walk to school, but we had to cross a river to get there. There was a bridge but it was miles away from where we were so Dad built us a flying fox with a box on it so we could sit two at a time and swing across the river. It was a lot of fun and surprisingly, no-one ever fell out and as far as I know it's still there.' She smiled at the thought. 'We went to a small country school at Tangarakau, which I doubt any of you would have heard of.'

'So, what years did you attend there then?' called Harvey from the back seat.

Sam swung around to see who had called out. '1947 to 1951,' she answered.

'I was there from 45 to 50,' smiled Harvey delightedly.

Sam took off the headset and stood up, placed it on the seat. 'Someone else can speak now, I think Harvey and I have some reminiscing to do,' she laughed.

'What was your maiden name?' he asked.

'Blackwell.'

'Ah yes, I remember, we used to call you Red Black because back then you had a mass of red curly hair.'

'That I did,' Sam laughed. 'It's all gone now though,' she ran her hand through her short-cropped strawberry coloured hair. 'Scooch over Mona, Harvey and I have a lot to catch up on.'

Jack was the next one to sit in the front seat

and don the headset.

'I also came from a big family,' he began. 'We lived in Wellington at the time, not dirt poor, but life wasn't easy either. I was the eldest of eight. As soon as I turned fifteen, I joined the Navy, decided I wanted to see the world,' he laughed. 'I loved Navy life and see a lot of the world I did. I wasn't too fussed about getting married or being a father, my father was no role model that's for sure, so the Navy life suited me.'

'A girl in every port eh?' said Bill glancing back at Jack through his rear-view mirror.

'Too right,' laughed Jack. 'Love em and leave em was my motto. 'I did fall in love with a lovely young girl once when I was on leave in Wellington. Trouble was, she wasn't in love with me. Came home from a stint at sea to find her in bed with someone else, so that put me right off women for a while.' He smiled ruefully. 'Anyway, I retired from the Navy, moved to Tauranga and became a tugboat captain. Retired from there a few years ago and moved to Rotorua where a couple of my brothers and sisters are now living. It's nice to be closer to family as you get older, especially as I live on my own.' He stood up, removed the headset and went a couple of seats down to let someone else sit in the front seat and tell their story.

This time it was Frank and Jan's turn. 'You speak for us both,' Frank said placing the headset on Jan's head.

'Oh, are you sure? Why don't you do the

talking?'

'Because you are the one who does all the talking in our household my love.'

'You cheeky blighter,' said Jan, but obviously not offended. She'd heard it all before. 'Okay then, if you insist. Well, where do I start. Frank and I met at high school; childhood sweethearts I guess you'd say. Frank and his brother came from a farming family in the Waikato, my family were orchardists, we grew apples and pears for the market back then. Anyway, when we got married, we lived in a small two room cottage on Frank's family farm until his dad died and then we moved into the smaller of the two homesteads. Franks brother was older and was expected to take over the farm, which he did, so he and his family moved into the main homestead. Frank and his brother ran the farm together for several years, they worked well together, made a good team. Frank's Mum lived with his brother in the big house, we had the smaller one to ourselves. We had our two children July and Frances while we were there. Once the kids were old enough to go to college, we moved off the farm and Frank got a job working as a stock buyer for Wrightson's until he retired about nine years ago. We've had a good life haven't we Frank?' Frank nodded. 'We've had our ups and downs like everyone else of course but all in all it's been pretty good.'

Frank took the headset off Jan's head and

spoke into the microphone. 'What Jan didn't tell you was that the reason I left the farm is because my brother and I had a major falling out. He wanted to turn our beautiful sheep and beef farm into a dairy farm and I was having none of it. He got his way in the end, and we left.' He put the headset back on the seat and went back to sit down a couple of rows back. Jan took Franks hand when they sat down, Tess couldn't help but notice the sadness on Frank's face and the tears in his eyes.

'Did they never heal the rift?' she pondered sadly.

By the time they got through the next few life stories Tess suggested they take another break and a toilet stop. She could see the pain etched on Bill's face as he gingerly rested his arm on his lap. He gratefully pulled over at a suitable spot and they got out to stretch their legs and relieve their bladders.

'I refilled the thermoses back at the Corner Store,' said Tess, who would like a cuppa?'

Everyone raised their hands, or their voices, so June helped Tess set up the table for the teas and coffees. They were barely an hour away from Tibooburra now, the last couple of hours had gone quickly, mostly due to the fact that they had been busy enjoying listening to each other's stories. Bill wandered around gently rubbing the nasty red swelling on his lower arm and wrist. One of the passengers had given him some Arnica cream to rub on it.

'Want some more pain killers?' Tess asked.

'Please,' he said.

Tess took her time packing up the picnic table giving Bill's pain relief time to work.

The only interesting thing along the last leg of their journey was the sad sight of a flat deck ute loaded with camping equipment broken down on the side of the road. Bill stopped to see if he could be of any help but was told there was a truck on its way from Tibooburra to pick them up.

'They're not going anywhere in a hurry,' sighed Bill climbing back into his seat, 'broken axle.'

Tibooburra was bigger than anyone expected. There was a large central business district and shopping area covering several streets, and they even had their own airport.

'Tibooburra was an old gold mining town, the name means 'heaps of rocks' in Aboriginal language,' explained Bill. 'There are a lot of significant Aboriginal sites in the area but unfortunately we don't have time to visit any of them on this trip'.

They pulled in to the Tibooburra Motel just before five o'clock, tired and weary. Bill began unloading the suitcases from the trailer with his one good arm while Tess went to reception to check in. Dinner would be at six o'clock, and a continental breakfast would be delivered to their rooms while they were having dinner. Once the keys were given out and everyone had set off to find their rooms, Tess went to see how Bill was getting on with the suitcases. One of the motel staff had seen him struggling with the suitcases and when he saw the swelling and bruising on Bill's arm, he took over and delivered the suitcases to the rooms, leaving Bill free to attend to the damaged trailer. It badly needed a wash and the inside needed a good sweep out, then of course the bus would need refuelling and cleaning out too, but Tess said she would help with that. Gus and

Frank came out and offered to help as well. Bill gratefully accepted their offer.

An expletive from Bill brought Tess running. She found him standing on the far side of the trailer scratching his head.

'What's the matter?' she asked as she walked around to see what he was looking at. There, lying on the ground, was the trailer wheel.

'When the last suitcase came out and the damn thing just fell off,' he said. 'If I can't get it fixed while we're here, we will have to stack the suitcases in the back seat.'

Tess left Bill, Gus and Harvey to carry on with what they had to do and went back to her room. She was pleasantly surprised to find that the units were clean and comfortable, but she suspected nobody would have cared if they weren't. She swept the dust off her suitcase and took it out of its plastic wrapping before taking it into her room, noting that the others were doing the same thing. It had been another long and interesting, day and Tess was looking forward to a quiet night and some much-needed rest. But life had other plans. Since arriving in Tibooburra, all the phone messages and emails Tess had missed for the past few days while they were out of signal range, were now sitting in her inbox waiting for a response. She made a coffee, got herself comfortable on the bed, plumped up her pillows, took a deep breath, and opened the first email.

Dinner was a relatively quiet affair, everybody was tired, happy but tired. They didn't have much to drink, preferring to have an early night. By seven thirty they began retiring to their rooms and within a very short space of time, the whole compound fell silent. A couple of the travellers took the opportunity to sit on the seats outside their units and enjoy the quiet and peace of the evening. Tess did the same, it was a beautiful end to another exciting day.

Day 11 - Tibooburra to Broken Hill

Tess was delighted to walk out the door of her unit next morning, into a beautiful warm, clear blue-sky day. She closed her eyes, raised her face to the rising sun and smiled.

'Perfect,' she thought, 'I love days like this.' She sat down at the small round table outside her door, with her toast and coffee. Most of the others were doing the same. Bill and the bus were nowhere to be seen. Tess had just finished reading through her notes for the day when the bus rolled into the compound and pulled up alongside the rooms. Bill hopped out and walked over to Tess and sat down on the chair on the other side of her table.

'Got a problem,' he said without formalities. 'Can't get the trailer wheel fixed so we will have to leave it here and load the luggage along the back seats.'

Tess noticed the swelling in Bill's arm had gone down but there was some pretty impressive bruising. She nodded to his arm.

'How is it?'

One of the passengers gave me some stuff called arnica and it's definitely made a difference,' he confessed. It's a lot better than it was, but I didn't get as much sleep as I would have liked because it was throbbing most of the night.'

'Have you had breakfast?'

Yep, the receptionist must have felt sorry for me, she rocked up to my room this morning with a big plate of bacon and eggs and some decent pain killers,' he admitted.

Three of the men from the group spotted Bill and came over to offer their assistance to stow the suitcases.

'I would appreciate that, thank you,' he said. 'No more trailer though I'm afraid, she's died on us, so we'll have to load them onto the back seats of the bus.'

The men looked at each other in surprise.

'Geez, that's gonna be a bit of a load for the old girl,' said Harvey, 'hope she can take it.'

'I hope so too, confessed Bill, 'guess we'll find out in due course.'

After they managed to cram all the suitcases in, the passengers were told they would have to bunch up for the rest of the journey.

'Sorry everyone, no more seats to yourselves.'

Bill was on the phone as Tess climbed into her seat.

'I've spoken to Jack, he said they could send someone up to meet us with another trailer if need be.'

'Are you going to do that?' asked Tess.

'I told him I'd see how she goes, hopefully we will at least make the 330kms to Broken Hill, I will make a decision then.'

Once everyone was on the bus, Tess informed her passengers that they would be having lunch at a roadhouse where sandwiches and savouries would be on offer for them. 'No more picnic lunches from here on,' she told them.

They bade farewell to their Tibooburra hosts and trundled out of the motel compound, turning south.

'This is what's known as the Silver City Highway,' announced Bill as he adjusted his headset. We will be on this highway until we reach Broken Hill.

'Why Silver City?' asked Sean.

'Broken Hill is also known as 'The Silver City' because of the silver mining there, hence the name of the highway.' He paused for a moment. 'Now Tess and I have decided that, seeing as you have all had to cram up with the back seat being unavailable, and the fact that it will be much easier travelling and a shorter day, we will stop more often to let you get out and stretch your legs. Our first stop will be at a rest area where there will be picnic tables and toilets. If you see something you want to have a closer look at or take a photo of just holler.'

The land was pretty dry and barren so there weren't any calls for Bill to pull over before they got to their morning tea stop. They pulled into a rest area seemingly out in the middle of nowhere. There was no one else at the stop, no vehicles to be seen in either direction and nothing much to be seen from one side of the horizon to the other.

Lena shuddered. 'This is a bit creepy, give me the city any day,' her voice sounded a little shaky.

'Nah, I'd much rather be out in the country,' said Gus, 'although, admittedly, this is a bit remote for me too.

Bill laughed, 'Come on you lot, we're only a couple of hundred kilometres from civilisation.'

'Yeah, but what if something happens and you need help?' asked Lena.

'See this nice piece of straight road here?' said Bill pointing up and down the highway, 'the Flying Doctors would be able to land there, pick you up and take you to the nearest hospital in no time at all. There is a Flying Doctor base in Broken Hill.' He paused for a moment then smiled at the group, 'besides there is always traffic along the highway, look, here comes a truck now.'

They stood clutching their hot drinks and munching on their biscuits as the truck came nearer and blew past them with a rumbling toot of his air horns. Not far behind the truck was a four-wheel drive vehicle towing a large caravan.

This time the vehicle pulled into the rest area and parked behind the bus. The driver and his passenger got out of their car, stretched and yawned and smiled at their audience. Some of the passengers had made their way further back off the road to scout around for wildflowers and mysterious insects. 'Watch out for snakes,' called Tess. She turned back to say hi to the newcomers.

'Where are you guys heading? she asked them.

'Tibooburra then Innamincka,' came the reply.

'We've just done that,' said Jenny, 'it was fabulous. Bit of a rough road though, not sure I would want to tow a caravan through there.'

The caravan owner smiled indulgently. 'We've been living on the road for a couple of years now and that beast there,' he said pointing to the caravan, 'is purpose built for the outback. It will take us anywhere we want to go,' he smiled proudly.

By now a couple of the men had gone across to check out the caravan. The owner was happy to show off his prized possession. Meanwhile his wife, having visited the ladies loo, came back and, accepting a cuppa from Tess, asked where they were from.

'New Zealand,' said Tess.

'Really?' the woman said, eyebrows raised. 'What part?'

'Mainly the middle of the North Island.'

'And Christchurch,' added Aggie.

'Yes, and Christchurch,' smiled Tess.

'I'm Elizabeth,' she said glancing around at the people standing around listening, 'my husband Chris and I are both from New Zealand, from Hamilton actually, but we've been travelling around Australia for the past two years. We absolutely love it, but I must admit we do miss the green, green grass of home sometimes,' she smiled wistfully.

Frank and Jan said they were from Hamilton too and the three of them started comparing notes, and not surprisingly, discovered they had acquaintances in common. The stop at the rest area lasted for about half an hour but while everyone was enjoying the break, Tess was happy to allow the extra time. If they got into Broken Hill a little later than planned, what did it matter.

The caravaners waved them off as they finally pulled out of the rest area and carried on down the Silver City Highway towards their lunch stop at Packsaddle Roadhouse. They hadn't gone far when there was a familiar explosion from beneath the bus.

'Damn,' said Bill, 'sounds like the replacement tyre has blown.' He got out to check and sure enough, the tyre he'd had replaced at Innamincka had blown out. They travelled on until they came to a small settlement called Mulgarinka which, thankfully, had a garage and they were able to get the tyre fixed. Bill took the opportunity to top up with fuel.

They were back on dirt roads again with short stretches of tar seal running from either side of the settlements they passed through. When they arrived at the Packsaddle Roadhouse there were a few other vehicles and several people either milling about or sitting on the veranda drinking beer.

'Didn't expect to see so many people way out here,' said June as they gathered their handbags and cameras before getting off the bus.

'There's accommodation and camp sites here,' said Bill, 'so you'd expect there to be a few people about. The grey nomads are more inclined to be on the move at this time of the year too, when the weather is a bit cooler.'

Once again, the passengers were in awe of the memorabilia adorning the walls and ceilings of the restaurant and bar. This time it was saddles, saddle bags and Akubra hats taking pride of place. While the group browsed around reading inscriptions and information notices, Tess went off to find someone to discuss their pre-booked lunch arrangements with. They were shown to a couple of tables beside the windows overlooking the parking area and their lunches were brought out on large platters. Once the platter was emptied and coffees and cakes had been dealt to, some of the visitors wandered out the back to take a look around the camping and accommodation areas.

They were pleasantly surprised at how inviting it was.

As they piled back on the bus June said, 'Gosh it's lovely here, wouldn't mind staying here for a few days.'

'Me neither,' agreed Mandy. Gus nodded his head too.

'Maybe we could stay here on another adventure,' smiled Tess, 'I will look into that idea.'

They drove off down the highway again, this time there were one or two calls for a photo stop along the way as they got closer to civilisation. At one point Bill pulled off unexpectedly and backed up the road a bit.

'What's up?' asked Tess.

'Echidna,' beamed Bill. 'Come on everyone,

come and have a look at this wee fella, they're one of my favourite animals.'

Everyone crowded excitedly off the bus and followed Bill across the road to where a spiny creature, not unlike a porcupine, was busy trying to bury himself in the dirt on the side of a bank.

'See his little feet working flat out,' said Bill. You can see that the back feet appear to be on backwards. That gives them the advantage of burrowing horizontally, watch.'

The cameras clicked and everyone stood around in awe as they watched the wee creature disappear into the bank.

'Wow, that was amazing,' exclaimed Sam. 'What a hardcase little character, looks a bit like a porcupine.'

'Echidnas and wombats are my favourites,' smiled Bill.

'Wombats? Can't say I've ever seen one of those,' mused Jan.

Just before they got to Broken Hill, they came across a roading crew with their accommodation camp set up close by.

'One thing I'll give the Aussies,' said Frank, 'they sure know how to build roads.'

'In a lot of places, they are able to build a temporary road adjacent to where they are working so the traffic can still flow unimpeded,' said Bill, 'but you need the right terrain to be able to do that, and Australia is one place where they can.'

They arrived at their accommodation in Broken Hill at around five o'clock, giving the passengers time to unpack for the next two nights and freshen up before heading to the bar adjacent to the restaurant for some pre-dinner drinks. Tess and Bill joined them there after they had gone over the next day's itinerary and made sure everyone had their suitcases and were settled into their rooms. There was only one hiccup, Lena didn't have any towels. The motel receptionist was most apologetic and sorted the issue out immediately.

The group were chatting so loudly the waitress had to shout to get their attention so she could tell them they were ready to take their meal orders in the dining room. Everyone got up and made their way to their table, drinks in hand. The chatting only stopped long enough for them to place their orders then away they went again. Bill looked across at Tess and gave her a wink and a smile. All was going well.

Day 12 – Broken Hill – The Silver City

The crows were in fine voice when Tess emerged from the best sleep she'd had in days. She lay back listening to them, she loved the cawing sound of the crows, it reminded her that she was in her second favourite country, Australia, New Zealand being her first of course. By the time she got herself organised and off to the restaurant for breakfast, everyone else was already there, including Bill.

'Morning sleepyhead,' he smiled. 'Looks like you had a good sleep, you look more relaxed than I've seen you since we started.'

Tess smiled back. 'How's the arm?'

'Much better thanks,' he said, proudly showing her the multi coloured bruising. 'Looks much worse than it is.

'Tess went over and poured herself a coffee, putting two slices of wholemeal toast in the toaster. 'We are on the home-stretch,' she said, sitting down and continuing their conversation, 'I feel I can relax a bit more now that it's almost over. Not that I'm glad it is coming to an end, but the pressure has come off a bit. We will be back in Adelaide tomorrow, not much can go wrong between now and then surely.'

'Let's hope not,' said Bill tucking into yet another sumptuous, cooked breakfast.

Tess laughed, 'I'll bet you've gained a few pounds since you started this trip,' she said eyeing his plate.

'I bet I have too,' he said, 'but to be honest, I really don't care. I have enjoyed the food and I have definitely enjoyed this trip Tess, I hope we can do this again sometime, it's been great.'

Tess placed a hand on top of Bill's, 'I can't thank you enough Bill, you have been an absolute Godsend and yes, I would very much like to do another trip with you too. I'm thinking about Adelaide to Darwin next year, would you be interested?'

'Too right I would,' he smiled broadly, 'keep me posted.'

'I will,' said Tess. She got up as the toaster popped and came back to the table with the toast, some butter pats and a small glass bowl of marmalade.

Some of the group lingered over their breakfast that morning, they didn't have to leave until nine o'clock, it was going to be a cruisy day. Others took the opportunity to go for a walk up the quiet streets to check out their surroundings and browse the shop windows.

Now that the suitcases had been off-loaded from the back seat, the passengers could spread themselves out again.

'Leave a seat at the front for our tour guide today please,' said Tess as she helped them aboard. They drove around to the Information Centre to pick up their local guide for the day. Tess and Bill got out of the bus to greet him. He outlined his plan for the day and they got back on the bus, the tour guide taking the front seat and Bill's headset.

'Morning everyone, my name is Barry, or Baz if you prefer, I respond to either,' he paused while everyone laughed. 'Welcome to The Silver City. Our first port of call this morning is the Line of Lode Miner's Memorial up on top of the hill, you might have seen it on your way in last night.'

A few people nodded. As Bill drove the bus up the hill Baz continued. 'The memorial is built on a mullock heap at the Line of Lode Reserve. Now that might all sound a bit double-dutch to you so I will explain. Mullock is waste from the mine and Line of Lode is the ore body that bisects the town. Now on your left here are the ruins of the BHP smelter and the old Delprat mine.'

He pointed out a huge oversized wooden park bench on top of the hill overlooking the city and asked if anyone wanted to have a photo taken on it. Several hands went up, so Bill pulled up alongside the seat while some of the passengers got out. There were a few strategically placed bricks which allowed the visitors to climb up onto the wooden construction. They said they felt like little kids sitting in an adult's chair. Tess knew the photos would look hilarious and requested Baz take her camera and get a snap of her sitting up there too. Continuing on around to the memorial, Baz showed Bill where to park and turned back to the passengers.

'Mining lies at the very heart of Broken Hill, and always has done – the town owes its very existence to Broken Hill Proprietary, which is now the world's largest mining company (BHP).' Turning to look out the window he continued. 'This impressive structure is a memorial to more than 800 miners who lost their lives here,' he said sombrely, 'the first deaths were due to lead poisoning. The miners were paid a lead bonus, but many believed the bonus was just a way to help produce insurance without admitting liability. It was meant to provide some capital for the family when the miner died. This was before the introduction of social welfare.'

Baz led the group through the daunting tunnel structure and into the shop and café area where people could sit by a window with a coffee and take in the view over the city or browse the shelves of memorabilia and appropriate souvenirs.

The group were very quiet and lost in their own thoughts as the bus made its way back down the hill from the memorial. Baz directed Bill to their next stop, the Silver City Mint and Art Centre.

'I think you will find this next stop pretty

amazing,' said Baz, 'I know I was impressed the first time I saw it; this is one of my favourite places. Just make your way into the main entrance there and follow the signs. You will eventually come to what is called 'The Big Picture', I won't tell you anymore about it, I will leave you to discover it for yourselves. I believe this is all paid for by Tess, is that right?' Baz looked across at Tess.

'Yes.' She nodded, 'please make sure you see everything. You will be given tickets as you go in, I will go and see to that now while you are getting off the bus.'

Baz led the group through the first few displays then left them to meander at their own pace once they got to the *Big Picture*. Tess followed them in and was blown away by the huge circular floor to ceiling artwork depicting the Australian Outback complete with flora and fauna. A wooden walkway allowed the viewers to walk around in front of the artwork and get a close up look at the detail. From there they followed their noses through various other silver, gem and artifacts displays before coming back out to the shop front where, once again, a large selection of souvenirs and silver jewellery were for sale and on display. Tess bought herself a pure silver ring, made right there in Broken Hill, it fitted perfectly on her ring finger.

'It's to ward off any unwanted attention,' she smiled at Bill as he looked over her shoulder.'

'Probably won't work,' he laughed. 'If a

bloke fancy's ya he's gonna try his luck anyway.'

They both laughed and wandered out to the bus to wait for the rest of the passengers.

Bill followed Baz's instructions to the Pro Hart Gallery on Wyman Street next.

'Pro Hart is one of Australia's famous icons,' said Baz as the bus came to a halt. This gallery of artwork will blow you away. It not only contains his own variety of works but also his collection of other famous artists works including Constable, Monet, Rembrandt and Picasso. The gallery has been left just the way it was when he died two years ago, in 2006. Even his famous Rolls Royce's are still here.'

Now, there's three levels to navigate so please take your time and hold on to the handrails. The artwork is for sale and there is also a gift shop in there so take your credit cards with you, and before you ask, no, I am not on commission,' he laughed as he led them off the bus.

'Gosh what an interesting place,' enthused June when she got back on the bus.

'And Pro Hart was certainly a very interesting man,' added Aggie.

'He was very talented wasn't he,' agreed Sam.

'Man, did you see what he did to that Rolls Royce out there in the shed,' exclaimed Jack as he clambered into his seat. 'He covered the whole damn thing in artwork.'

Sam wasn't quite sure whether Jack was impressed or appalled, and she wasn't about to ask, she thought it looked great.

'Morning tea stop next,' said Baz as the remaining passengers got back on the bus. 'Bill, would you kindly take us back to the Information Centre please.' Turning back to the group he said, 'We have a wonderful café there, you can get yourselves something to eat and drink before we head off again.'

When the passengers got off the bus and entered the building, Baz showed them through the centre before directing them to the café. An impressive souvenir shop was strategically placed close to the café drawing a lot of attention from the travellers, by the time they left some of them had purchased several souvenirs and gifts to take home.

'The Albert Kersten Mining and Minerals Museum, or Geo Centre, is next on the list,' said Baz, settling himself back in his front seat and turning to face the passengers. 'It is a representation of the mineral history of Broken Hill, as is the building it is in, the old Bond Store which was built back in 1892. Inside you will discover the history of the planet and learn about the region's geology. It includes the science of crystals and how the minerals are formed and extracted. It might sound boring but believe me, I think you will find it fascinating. Keep an eye out for the forty-two-kilogram nugget and the Silver Tree, each of them has a very interesting story to tell.'

Baz hopped off the bus and helped the passengers down the steps while Tess went in to pay the entrance fee.

The passengers didn't linger here as long as they did in the previous places they had visited but they did agree that it was interesting and well worth the visit.

The Royal Flying Doctor Service was next. They pulled up outside the RFDS building and the passengers filed through the main entrance, stepping right into its history. They spent some time walking through the museum before being guided to a theatre to watch a fifteen-minute film about the RFDS. This was followed by a walk through the hangar to check out the various aircraft and to ask questions of the staff.

Most of the group purchased a memento from the shop before they left, knowing that the money they spent would be going to a worthy cause. Tess chose a red water bottle with the words *Royal Flying Doctor Service* printed on the side in silver.

'Hope you enjoyed that,' said Baz as they left the RFDS building. There was collective affirmation from everyone.

'Must be a very rewarding job, being a Flying Doctor, or Nurse,' said June. 'Just imagine being stuck way out in the sticks needing help and seeing that lovely plane coming in knowing medically trained people were on board.'

'I liked that sign that said,' Mandy glanced down at a piece of paper in her hand, 'The far-off boundary rider – the lonely drover's wife, deserved to be protected, kept in touch, given a go and it took a man like John Flynn to make it so. It was written by Ted Egan, whoever he was.'

'Ted Egan worked with the Department of Aboriginal Affairs and spent a lot of his time in the bush as a stock worker and even did some crocodile hunting during his time as a patrol officer and reserve superintendent,' Baz informed them. 'He also taught in bush schools and was a sole teacher at the Newcastle Waters Station in 1965 when the creek flooded and they were stranded for six weeks, so he certainly knows how valuable the Flying Doctor Service is. On top of that he was a well-known musician for most of his adult life. As for John Flynn, you will have heard and read a lot about him in the museum. He certainly was a remarkable man, and many people owe their lives to him.' Baz looked at his watch, 'We are off to the world-famous metropolis of Silverton next,' he smirked. 'Anyone been there before?' Nobody responded so he continued. 'Anyone seen Mad Max two with Mel Gibson, or Razorback or A Town like Alice?' he asked again.

This time a few hands went up. 'Great,' enthused Baz, 'today you will see where those movies were made.'

There was a buzz of excitement as they headed out of town. A couple of kilometres down the road Baz leant over and gave Bill some directions. Bill followed the instructions and brought the bus to a stop beside a large outcrop of white quart rocks.

'What on earth is that white cart doing way out here?' asked June.

'That's what I am about to talk to you about,' smiled Baz. 'Hop off and go have a look at it while I tell you the story of *The Battle of Broken Hill*.' He waited until everyone, including Bill and Tess, had gathered round. 'Every New Year's Day the Unity Lodge of Goodfellow would host a picnic for the townsfolk. The picnic was always held in Silverton so they would travel there by train. However, on the first of January 1915, the excursion took a tragic turn. Living in the town at the time were two Muslim cameleers from India. When they gave up working with camels, one of them, Mahommed Gool, became an ice-cream vendor. This is a replica of his ice cream cart. The other man, Mullah Abdullah became a butcher. Gool was well known around the town as he went around in his ice cream cart, but on this particular day in 1915, he used the cart to transport himself and Mullah out here for sinister purposes. Apparently, these men had an axe to grind. It is said that several days prior to this date, Abdullah had been convicted by the Police Court for slaughtering sheep on premises not licensed for slaughter, he was a butcher remember. Anyway, this was not his first offence by all accounts. Also, several years before that, he had stopped wearing his turban because 'some larrikin threw stones at me and I did not like it.' Sounds like the man might have held a bit of a grudge. Now on the day of the picnic, twelve hundred men, women and children crowded themselves onto forty open ore rail trucks. Gool and Abdullah, in the meantime, had positioned themselves on an embankment close to the train tracks and waited. When the train with its open rail trucks came into view the two men opened fire. They managed to fire off twenty to thirty shots.'

There was a gasp from the gathered group. 'Oh my Lord,' said Lena, visibly disturbed, 'that's dreadful, those poor people. Was anybody hurt?'

'Sadly yes,' replied Baz. 'Initially the passengers thought the shots were in honour of the train's passing or that it was a make-believe fight for entertainment, but once people started falling, the reality of the situation sunk in. A young seventeen-year-old girl, Alma Cowie, was the first to die, followed by William Shaw whose daughter Lucy was injured. Then came Mary Kavanagh, George Stokes, Thomas Campbell, Alma Crocker, Rose Crabb and Constable Robert Mills. Their names all appear here on this plaque.'

'So, were they caught?' asked Jan? 'What happened next?'

'Well, the two men made a run for it while the train carried on to a siding where they telephoned for help. The Police arrived and went in pursuit of Gool and Abdullah. They found another dead body, a chap named Alfred Millard, who had been sheltering in his hut. They eventually tracked the pair near the Cable Hotel and that's where they shot and wounded Constable Mills. They ran off and took shelter here, at this outcrop, it provided them with good cover for the ninety-minute battle that was to follow. In the end very little shooting was coming from the two men. Abdullah was dead but Gool stood with a white rag tied to his rifle. This was ignored and he was gunned down. They said later that he had sixteen wounds. The mob surrounding the bodies wouldn't allow the bodies to be taken away in an ambulance, instead they were disposed of in secret by the Police. There was another victim, James Craig who lived in a house behind the Cable Hotel. He ignored his daughter's warning about chopping wood during a gun battle and was hit by a stray bullet.'

The group stood quietly with their own thoughts.

'Did they ever figure out why they did it?' asked Sam.

'There was a lot of conjecture of course,' offered Baz, 'but Gool did have a note tucked in his belt which stated that he was a subject of Ottoman Sultan and that '*I must kill you and give my life for my faith, Allahu Akbar*'. Abdullah also left a letter, so the story goes, his one said he was dying for his faith and in obedience to the order of the Sultan, '*but owing to my grudge against the Chief Sanitary inspector Brosnan it was my intention to kill him first*'. Brosnan was the man who brought the charges against Abdullah.' Baz glanced at his watch. 'Time we moved on,' he said. 'We have a date with old Lofty Cannard, the camel man.

'Oooh I was hoping we would get to see some camels up close,' enthused Lena. 'I heard they smell bad,' she giggled, 'is that right?'

'I guess you are about to find out,' laughed Baz. 'One of the guides used to say that if you wanted to go for a ride on a camel you had to get there early otherwise you will end up with the ugly ones.' Everyone roared with laughter.

They pulled up just outside the fenced off area and walked slowly and quietly onto the compound. Several Camels were standing or lying about lazily chewing their cud. Lofty came wandering out, greeted Baz and turned to the group. He talked about the camel trek operation he had been running for more than fifty years, and about his love of the animals.

'Why do they smell so bad?' asked Mandy wafting her hand under her nose to ward off the smell.

'It's the cud they chew,' answered Lofty. 'These camels have three stomachs, they eat their food, it goes into one stomach, passes through into another stomach where it ferments and is then regurgitated and chewed on to make it palatable for the third stomach. At least that is what I am told. And before you ask, why do camels have humps,' he paused and smiled at the group, 'these humps are what allows a camel to survive for long periods of time in the desert without food and water. A full, healthy hump can weigh up to thirty-five kilograms but when it is depleted it will shrink down and sometimes fold over.'

A few of the travellers followed Lofty over to take a closer look at the animals, the rest preferred to keep a safe distance between them and the interesting but smelly creatures.

When they got back on the bus, Jan recalled that she had read a book called *Tracks* a year or two back. It's about a young woman who walk across the desert with some camels and a dog.'

'Ah, yes,' said Baz, I know it well, it was a true story. The woman's name is Robyn Davidson, I think she came from Brisbane. Anyway, she developed a deep love and appreciation for camels when she got a job back in the 1970's working for a cameleer. Eventually she decided she wanted to escape from life for a while and walk across the desert with her dog and some camels. It's quite a story, I highly recommend it. Bill, would you stop here for a minute while I tell everyone about this metropolis in front of us,' he said with a cheeky grin. 'This is what I call the real Outback, and Silverton is a real deal Outback town. As you can see, it has lovely old stone buildings, wide dusty streets and it has a population you can count on your fingers. It was a thriving hub for a short time in the 1800's with a population of around three thousand at its peak. Then that fellow Charles Rasp, found a large silver deposit and everything changed. Although there are only a handful or residents left there now, we do get more than one hundred and twenty thousand tourists through here every year. That popularity has arisen mainly from the movies that were made here. Remember I asked you whether you had seen *Mad Max 2* and *A Town like Alice* and *Razorback*? Well, this is where it all happened.'

Bill turned off the road onto the wide dirt road and parked outside the Silverton Hotel. There in all its glory stood the *Mad Max 2* car.

'Wow is that the actual car they used in the movie?' asked Jack.

'Sure is,' beamed Baz proudly. 'And around the side of the hotel you will find dozens of boards with various hotel names on them, the name of this hotel changed with each movie. Go on inside the pub and have a look around, there are a lot of funny stories and jokes plastered all over the place which will amuse you. Grab yourselves a drink and meet me out the side there under the veranda when you are ready. That's where we will be having lunch and that's also where the toilets are.'

Baz wandered off to find the hotel proprietor to sort out lunch. By the time everyone had made their way from inside the pub and found a seat at the long wooden table outside under the veranda, their lunch was sitting on large platters waiting for them. There was a lot of loud chatter and laughter as the group shared what they had seen inside the pub.

'There's a lot of memorabilia in there from the Mad Max movie,' said Jack enthusiastically. 'I was a great fan of those movies. Can't remember what year Mad Max 2 was though, somewhere around 1980 wasn't it?'

'1981 to be exact Jack. Yes, I was a fan too. There's been a lot of movies made out here, as you can see by all these boards with hotel names on them,' he said, gesturing to the boards on the wall and still more piled up against the walls. 'Remember that movie, *Priscilla Queen of the Desert*?' Most of them did. 'Well, that was filmed here in 1994. *Razorback* was ten years earlier in 1984 and did you know that the TV series *The Flying Doctors* was also filmed here? That was from 1986 to 1993. I loved that show. Did you get it in New Zealand?'

'We did,' smiled Lena, it was one of my favourites.'

'Mine too agreed Aggie.'

When they reluctantly dragged themselves away from the Silverton Hotel, Baz got Bill to drive around the rest of the wide dirt streets to have a look at some of the well maintained, iconic stone buildings. As they got back to the main road Baz announced that they were headed to the Mundi Mundi Lookout.

When they got there, they piled out of the bus and stood beside Baz as he drew their attention to the long straight road they could see stretching way into the distance below them.

'That's one of the drawcards for movie producers,' he beamed 'and you can see why. It's a perfect location for so many scenarios.'

'This is where Priscilla would have been riding on top of that bus in all his or her glory,' laughed Mandy. 'I watched that movie so many times I lost count.'

'All I see is dead stuff,' bemoaned Lena.

'Not so,' said Tess defensively. 'You would be amazed at how much life there is out there.'

'That's true,' agreed Baz, 'this place is teeming with life. 'If we had the time, I would take you down there and show you. As a matter of fact, this is Mundi Mundi Station,' he said waving his arm around to indicate the surrounding area, 'and it carries about ten thousand sheep believe it or not.'

After taking copious amounts of photos, including a group photo courtesy of Baz, they climbed back on the bus.

'Next stop is the Living Desert and Sculptures,' announced Baz. 'Lena, this will show you how much life there actually is out there in the desert, I think you will be surprised. With regard to the sculptures, I will tell you more about these when we get there, they are really something. Not what you would expect to find way out here in the desert but that's probably what makes them so spectacular.'

They made their way out to the Living Desert and drove through the gates.

'This Living Desert is a flora and fauna sanctuary, covers a hundred and eighty hectares, and is bordered by a predator-proof fence,' stated Baz.

'Oh look,' exclaimed Jan, there's a Kangaroo.'

'Actually, that is a rock wallaby,' smiled Baz. 'But with any luck you might see a red kangaroo.'

'What's the difference between a wallaby and a kangaroo?' asked Sam

'A wallaby is smaller than a kangaroo and lives in a variety of terrains. For example, this one we just saw was a rock wallaby because it lives here amongst the rocks but there are also brush, swamp, forest and shrub wallabies. Wallaroos and kangaroos vary in size with some of the male reds growing as tall as six feet. I believe one has been measured at almost seven feet tall, now that would be a force to be reckoned with. If you ever see two big male reds fighting you will see that they use their large feet more than their paws.

They are a formidable enemy if you decided to take one on. Not something I would recommend,' he laughed. 'One of the reasons kangaroos get hit by vehicles on the road is because of those long feet, they can't turn around in a hurry and they can't back up either. One thing they can do though is jump. Their legs work a bit like a rubber band, the Achilles tendon stretches as the animal comes down then releases its energy to propel the kangaroo forward in the bouncing motion that some of you may have seen.'

'There's one,' called Mandy excitedly.

Bill stopped the bus and they all sat quietly watching.

'Perfect timing,' laughed Baz. 'You can see how they bounce along. It is said they can leap as far eight or nine metres in a single bound and can reach speeds of up to sixty kilometres an hour.'

'Wow,' said Jack oozing admiration, 'I never knew any of that. That's damned impressive.'

Bill drove on up to a parking area under Baz's guidance and stopped the bus.

'Here beside us on this hill are the Living Desert Sculptures. Has anyone heard about these?' Nobody had so Baz continued. 'In 1993 an artist by the name of Lawrence Beck directed and organised a sculpture symposium here with twelve different sculptors from around the world including Georgia, Mexico, Syria, Bathurst Island and Australia. Beck was from Gosford. They brought in fifty-three tonnes of sandstone to here, from Wilcannia. They started work on the 1st of April, and that's no joke,' laughed Baz. 'They finished in the third week of May. This whole area was transformed into an artwork of international standing and hey presto, Broken Hill proudly had a new icon. Broken Hill City Council provided most of the funding for it and they were impressed with the outcome. So, let's go and take a walk and have a closer look at these sculptures shall we? There are plaques beside each one with all the details.'

As everyone made their way up the stone paths to the sculptures Baz, Tess and Bill stayed back to talk.

'That esky I got you to put in the back of the bus has got some bottles of champagne, orange juice and snacks in it. If you think your group might enjoy it, and are not too tired, we could sit up here for a little while and watch the sun go down. The sculptures are even more impressive with the setting sun shining through them, it's just an optional extra. I leave the decision up to the tour hosts at this point, you know your passengers better than I do. The younger groups jump at the chance of course, but your group might prefer to get back to their motel rooms and rest up before dinner.'

Tess looked at Bill. 'What do you think?' Then turning to Baz, 'We aren't far from town are we? We could be back at the motel within what, half an hour?'

'Yes, give or take,' Baz replied.

Tess turned back to Bill. He in turn looked up the hill and watched the group as they meandered slowly amongst the sculptures, stopping to read the inscriptions as they went.

'I reckon they might enjoy that,' said Bill.

'I agree,' said Tess. 'We don't have to wait until its dark do we, just long enough to enjoy a drink and some nibbles and a bit of quiet reflection? Yes, let's do it.'

Baz beamed. 'Was hoping you would,' he said, 'I didn't want to influence you at all, but this is a really nice way to end the day.'

Tess left the two men to set up while she went and took some video and photos of the sculptures, the lighting was perfect.

As people started making their way back down the path in dribs and drabs, they were offered a glass of champagne or orange juice and a selection of snacks. Their faces lit up at the surprise offerings and their smiles broadened.

'Well, this is a lovely surprise,' said Mandy.

'Most unexpected,' added Gus. 'Thank you. What's the occasion?'

'Who needs an occasion,' said Baz, 'let's just celebrate the day.'

By the time everyone had arrived back at the bus the sun was getting closer to the horizon. They all found comfortable flat stones to perch on and quietly watched the sun in its descent.

'This is perfect,' sighed Aggie as she put an arm around her sister's shoulder. Thank you so much for encouraging me to come on this trip Sis, it has been absolutely marvellous.'

June leaned into Aggie's embrace and said, 'I am so glad I did too, it has been wonderful sharing all this with you. We must do it again.'

'Yes we must,' agreed Aggie.

'Here's to Baz, thank you for a fantastic day,' said Frank as he raised his glass to their guide.

'Here, here,' came the responding chorus.

'And I would like to raise a glass to Tess and Bill while we are at it,' Doug said as he got to his feet. 'This has been the most exciting, informative and entertaining trip Jenny and I have ever done and if you are planning another adventure like this in the future, count us in.'

'And us,' added Frank and Jan.

'Me too,' said Sam, this has been thee best trip ever.'

And so the accolades continued until everyone had had their say and silence fell again. Tess had tears in her eyes and when she sneaked a glance at Bill, she could see him swallowing hard as well. Yes, it had been a very rewarding trip so far, but it wasn't over yet.

On the way back to Broken Hill they spotted an old Aboriginal man sitting under the shade of a tree and a wild camel just wandering along the roadside minding its own business.

They dined out at the Democrats Club that night and between laughter, wine, beers and pokie machines, they all had a great night out. They were pretty buzzed up by the time they got back to their motel units.

'Another successful day done and dusted,' Tess said to Bill as she bade him goodnight. 'How did it go today, do you think we'll make it to Adelaide without a trailer?'

'So far she seems to be doing okay,' said Bill cautiously. 'Fingers crossed we'll make it to Adelaide. Have a good night Tess, see you in the morning.'

'Night Bill,' she said, as she let herself into her room. She made a coffee, grabbed the remote and turned on the tele. They were back in

civilisation, it was time to catch up on the news of
the world again.

Bill was up bright and early next morning, cleaning out the bus, refuelling and getting ready for the long day ahead. He would normally have done all that the night before but by the time they got back from the previous day's outing, there wasn't much time before they were heading off to dinner, so he decided to get a good night's sleep and get up early in the morning.

Tess was also up early catching up on paperwork. At breakfast she suggested the passengers might like to grab some snacks from the vending machines at reception or from the local store just up the road. If need be, they would stop at a store on the way out of town.

'It's a long way to Adelaide and not much in the way of civilisation along the way,' she'd told them. 'There is a roadhouse but I believe it may have just gone out of business, so we don't want to take any chances. Bill has put a new slab of water on the bus for us so don't worry about buying bottles of water.'

Tess spotted Bill carting the suitcases onto the bus to stack them once again along the back seat. She went over to help.

'Thanks Tess,' said Bill, hand me those bigger ones first, then I'll stack the smaller ones around them.' He got out of the bus. 'Right, how are we going for time? It's nearly three hours' drive to Wentworth, do you want to do a late morning tea there or an early lunch?

Tess studied her watch. 'Let's play it by ear,' she said, 'see how everyone is. What is it, six hundred kilometres to Adelaide?'

'Bit more than that,' said Bill, 'but it won't seem that long on these straight roads, not like it did out on the desert tracks.

'Tess nodded. 'Well, we are on the homeward stretch now, can't say I'm sorry about that in a way. It's been a fantastic trip but I'm starting to get a bit weary and if I'm getting tired, I wonder how the passengers are coping?'

'I'm used to long days on the road,' said Bill, 'but I have to admit I'm getting a bit weary on it too.'

They were on the road just after eight o'clock. Everyone seemed to be in good spirits, just not as spritely and energetic as they had been at the start of the trip.

'Everyone okay this morning?' she asked as they made their way out of Broken Hill.

There was a consensus of agreement that they were all good.

'Mixed feelings really,' said Jan. 'Looking forward to getting home, but not wanting the trip to end. Sounds silly I know, but that's how I feel.'

'I think you speak for most of us Jan,' said Sam. I feel a bit the same way. Still, it's not over yet we still have today and tomorrow before we fly home.'

Tess left the group to chat. She had prepared a list of questions about the trip from day one, as Bill had suggested a few days ago. She would pull it out when she felt her passengers might appreciate a bit of fun. For now though, there was plenty to see out the windows.

At ten o'clock they stopped at a roadside rest area and set up for morning tea and a toilet break. There wasn't much to see so as soon as they had finished their drinks and been to the loo, they reboarded the bus again. Along this leg of the journey Tess pulled out her questionnaire and started asking questions to see how much they had retained of their trip.

'What was the name of the bus driver who picked us up from the airport in Adelaide?' was her first question. There was silence for a moment before Aggie piped up and said, 'Slim?'

'Correct,' said Tess. 'What was the name of the motel we stayed in in Adelaide?'

Silence again except for a bit of rustling of paper as someone searched in their bag for the letter she had sent them with all their flight and accommodation details on it.

'The Comfort Inn,' cried Mona delightedly.

And so the questions continued, at times bringing forth memories and tales of their experiences.

Bill drove them around Wentworth and down to the junction where the Murray and Darling Rivers met.

'What are those boats moored along the side of the river?' asked Frank.

'Houseboats,' said Bill, pulling to a stop so they could have a closer look. 'You can hire them and go cruising up and down the Murray River. I did it once with a couple of friends of mine, it was a fantastic trip, highly recommend it,' he said enthusiastically.

Jan looked at Frank and said, 'Write that down, I would love to do that, wouldn't you?'

Frank nodded in agreement. 'We could go with the Freeman's, they'd like it too I reckon.'

Bill cruised on through town and pulled up outside the Information Centre and went in. When he came out, he was carrying a small book and a piece of paper. Without a word he drove further on and stopped outside Fotherby Park. He had a huge smile on his face and Tess wondered what he was up to. He turned in his seat to face the passengers.

'In this park, is something I reckon you Kiwis will really get a kick out of. It's a statue of a Kiwi bloke named David Jones. Ever heard of him?'

Nobody had, so he suggested they all get out and have a look at the statue and he would enlighten them on the story of David James (Jimmy) Jones. As they gathered around the diminutive bronze figure Bill opened up the book, took out the piece of paper wedged inside it, and looked up at them.

'Many years ago, I read this book called 'A Man Called Possum,' he said waving the book in the air. I've never forgotten it and I thought you might appreciate this man's story as he was from New Zealand. He was born in Ruapuna, south of Christchurch in 1901 and came to Aussie in 1927 and went to work as a shearer. He was an accomplished shearer and he was in demand, and for a while he was almost fully employed. Unfortunately, the Great Depression was starting to bite by 1929 and his work was drying up. He applied several times for the newly introduced sustenance relief fund called 'the susso' but was refused each time. He felt it was probably because he was a New Zealander and he also understood that any jobs that became available would go to the locals first. This caused him to lose heart so he took to the bush, rejected society, and lived like a hermit. He would borrow newspapers out of peoples letterboxes then return them when he'd read them, even if it was a day or two later. He did everything he could to avoid coming into contact with people. He spent most of his time along the Murray and Darling rivers and it is believed he travelled from Mannum in the west to Red Cliffs in the east and north up the Darling to Wilcannia. He would walk at night and could cover up to 50kms. He set up camps along the river and would use them as he went back and forth. He never accepted offers of shelter or food from anyone. He slept in the bush mostly, taking shelter in abandoned buildings, pump houses, chicken sheds or hay sheds if it was wet. He got the name 'Possum' because he sometimes slept in trees. If he saw something that needed fixing or attending to during his travels, he would tend to it. One thing he did that the farmers were not happy about was that Jimmy hated seeing dogs chained up and if he came across any he would set them free.'

This brought forth gales of laughter from the group. They were hanging onto Bill's every word. He continued with his story. 'The only charity Jimmy would accept were gifts of shoes and clothing which the farmers would leave in the bush where he would find them. He lived off the land and never raided a vege garden unless it was big enough that the farmer might not miss one or two items. If he did take any food from the gardens, he always did a chore for the farmer in return. It was even recorded that he was known to climb trees to raid beehives, he must have had a sweet tooth,' laughed Bill.

'Did nobody ever try and help the poor man?' asked Lena plaintively.

'Yes, many times,' said Bill. 'In fact, there was one Policeman that Jimmy would talk to and he tried to do what he could for him but Jimmy refused most of the help offered to him. He was offered the pension on several occasions but he refused saying he hadn't worked and paid taxes, so he didn't consider he was entitled to it. They tried to make things easy for him to apply but he kept refusing, he even went to prison for vagrancy a couple of times rather than fill out any paperwork. It was a pretty tough life by all accounts, not only because he lived off the land but also because of all the weather events and extremes of weather he had to contend with. He went through droughts, floods, and dust storms. Day time temperatures could range from 40ºC to nearly zero at night. As he got older, he became unwell, his eyesight was failing and he'd lost most of his teeth so eating became a problem. When he was sixty, his policeman friend gave him some glasses so he could still read the newspapers. On a cold winters day in 1982, they found Jimmy propped up against a tree at Ned's Corner Station between Wentworth and Renmark. They estimated he had passed away about four weeks earlier, he was eighty-one years old. He had lived alone in the bush for fifty-four years.'

'That is so sad,' said Lena, a tear in her eye. 'I wonder why he never went home?'

'I guess we'll never know,' said Bill. 'Despite the fact that he shunned society, a hundred and eighty people turned up to his funeral. Everyone knew about him and loved him, but I guess he died never knowing that. If anyone wants to read the full story, we can whip back to the Information Centre so you can get yourselves a copy.'

A couple of hands went up, so Bill got them back on the bus and took them off to get a copy of 'A Man Called Possum'. Four of them got out at the Information Centre, the rest sat on the bus and waited.

'Remember that trip we did with you Tess when we went on the Murray Princess up the Murray River. Gosh that was a great trip,' enthused June as they waited.

'It was June, I remember it well,' agreed Tess. 'The only thing I didn't appreciate was that I ended up being put in a tiny room right beside the generator and hardly got any sleep for the three nights we were on the river.'

'I remember you got quite merry on champagne that last night at dinner and got up and sang with the entertainer,' laughed June.

'In my defence I was invited up to sing, and I didn't have much to drink, I was just very tired. Anyway, less said about that the better. What goes on tour stays on tour June, you know that.' Tess said, grinning at her.

The book buyers came back with Bill and got on board proudly showing off their purchases.

Once they'd had left the outskirts of Wentworth and there wasn't so much to see, Tess continued on with her trip questions. Everything was going fine for until Bill made a noise that sounded like a groan, causing Tess's blood to run cold.

'Everything alright?' she asked taking in the tense expression on his face.

'I'm afraid not,' he said quietly. 'Something doesn't feel right with the old girl, I think the engine might be packing up.'

The words were no sooner out of his mouth than the engine stopped dead. Bill steered the bus off the road and let it roll to a stop amongst the shrubs and trees along the roadside. He leaned forward and put his head on the steering wheel. Then he sat up, rubbed his face and took a deep breath. He glanced across at Tess and shrugged before turning to face the passengers sitting very still and quiet in the back, looking very concerned.

'What's up?' asked Jack.

'I think the extra load with the suitcases might have done her in,' said Bill sadly as he got out of the bus and went to have a look at the engine. He came back to Tess.

'I need to phone the depot and see if we can get a replacement bus sorted. We aren't going anywhere in this old girl,' he said sadly as he pulled out his phone. He frowned when he saw he had no reception. 'I'm going to get up on top of that hill over there and see if I can get some reception. The only other option is for me to get a ride to Mildura with someone and leave you guys here.'

Tess watched Bill cross the road and clamber up the hill waving is phone around trying to get a signal. Finally, he came back down to the bus.

'Managed to get hold of Jack back at the depot, is going to get a replacement bus sent up from Wentworth,' he said. 'Nothing much else we can do until it gets here.'

He turned to ask the passengers if everyone was okay and laughed out loud when he saw that they had gone ahead off their own bat, hauled out the foldout picnic table, and started setting up for another morning tea.

'Here, let me help you with that,' said Bill moving towards them.

'Nope,' they said, 'this one's on us. 'It's about time we did something for you for a change, how do you have your coffee.'

'Black with one,' he replied, 'and thank you. 'There's a replacement bus on its way from Wentworth so we could be stuck here for a wee while.' He looked around at their surroundings. 'There's some handy toilet-trees over there, he smiled, 'and we still have loo paper on board so hopefully that covers all our needs for now.'

'Don't worry about us Bill, we know everything is going to be fine, it's all part of the adventure,' said Sam cheerfully.

As they wandered off to check out the wildflowers and fauna, Bill called after them to watch out for snakes. Tess, clutching her coffee in one hand, leaned back on the bus beside Bill and smiled at her group.

'They never cease to amaze me,' she said. 'Nothing seems to bother them; they just take everything in their stride.'

'As an *older* person,' said Bill with a twinkle in his eye, 'I have to admit that as you get older you tend not to give a damn as much as you did when you were younger. Dunno, seems the closer we get to God the less we have to fear.'

Tess laughed. 'Guess I've yet to find that out. Truth is though, I would much rather travel with Seniors than any other age groups. They are just so much easier to deal with and so much fun, as you have seen for yourself.'

'I've never travelled with a group of Kiwi's before, you guys are my first, and hopefully not my last,' he added. 'I've really enjoyed this trip.'

'Me too, and a lot of that is down to you Bill, I'm glad we had you for our driver. I think I've already told you that, but I mean it.'

'Awww shucks,' laughed Bill obviously pleased with the compliment. 'So, do you not take any other age groups on tours then?'

Tess laughed. 'Nope. But having said that, I have taken some fifty to sixty-year-olds now and again and lived to regret it.'

'How so?' Bill was intrigued.

Tess put her cup back on the picnic table, folded her arms and leaned back against the bus as she told Bill some stories about the 'younger' people she had taken on tour.

'I do have a blacklist of people I will never travel with again,' she confessed, 'there's no second chances with me, if people want to be disruptive or cause trouble then they can travel with someone else. I sometimes wonder if I have inherited some of those people from other companies' blacklists,' she sighed, then turned and grinned at Bill. 'It's all part of the job though isn't it.'

Bill nodded in agreement. 'Yes, as my Scottish aunt used to say, *there's nought so queer as folk.*'

Tess threw back her head and laughed heartily, 'Love it,' she said, I must remember that one.' She looked around to check on where everyone was. They seemed content enough just standing around in groups chatting, or walking around heads down, studying what was under their feet.

'Have you every sent anyone home?' asked Bill, picking up the conversation again.

'Once or twice. One poor old dear was clearly not very agile when we picked her up. It became clear early on that she wasn't going to be able to handle a big South Island tour, and she realised it too so, by mutual agreement, we put her on a bus to go back home. I felt really bad for her but she seemed to take it in her stride, I think she was relieved to be honest. Another time we did ask one woman why she was on the trip, and did she want to go home because she was so grumpy and bad tempered. I felt awful when her eyes filled up with tears though. She said it was her first trip, her husband had died a couple of years earlier, and she had never travelled on her own. Poor thing was way out of her comfort zone. I had a chat with a couple of the other ladies travelling on their own and they kindly took her under their wing and she ended up having a wonderful time. In fact, she came on a couple more trips after that.'

'I guess you could write a book about your experiences,' said Bill.

'No doubt you could write one about yours too,' responded Tess.

'True, although as a driver I am all care no responsibility.

'I'll bet it's not, if you really think about it,' smiled Tess knowingly, 'there must have been a lot of things you've seen and done over the years that would be of interest to someone who has never travelled or seen the Outback.'

Bill was thoughtful for a moment, then he smiled. 'You know what, you might be right about that, I guess I take a lot for granted. I have never thought what I did was anything out of the ordinary but maybe there is a story or two to tell.'

There was a shout from one of the

travellers.

'Here comes the bus.'

The replacement Coaster bus from Wentworth rolled up and parked behind Bill's bus. The driver, Terry, introduced himself and suggested Tess get everyone on board while he and Bill loaded the suitcases in the luggage trailer hooked on behind his bus.

They were all packed up and on their way within fifteen minutes. The group were sad to leave their old bus behind, they had grown fond of it, they had shared some great experiences with that bus.

It wasn't far to Mildura and, at Tess's request, Terry cruised the main streets pointing out cafes for the passengers to go and get themselves some lunch. The beautiful clear blue sky was now filling up with ominous darkening clouds but, as yet no rain.

Tess requested they try and cut their lunch break down to half an hour.

'We still have another four or five hours to go before we get to Adelaide.'

An hour and a half later they crossed over the bridge spanning the Murray River and rolled into Renmark.

'There's more of those houseboats,' called Jan excitedly. 'Frank, we really must look seriously at doing that, it looks so quiet and peaceful down there.'

They cruised through Renmark and

stopped down by the river for a brief toilet stop before continuing on to Adelaide, their final destination.

The last three hours of the trip seemed to last forever and the group were very quiet as they travelled the last hundred kilometres, tiredness was really setting in. At least they were back on tar seal, but it had begun to rain again. The roadsides were greening up with all the rain, providing a more interesting landscape, but many had nodded off and missed it. Even Bill, who was sitting beside Tess in one of the front seats, dozed off. She felt sorry for him, it had been a long tiring journey and he wasn't a young man. She rested her head back on the headrest and gazed out the window. She woke herself up sometime later as her head jerked back from lolling on her chest. She wiped the dribble from her mouth and looked around to make sure nobody had seen her fall asleep.

They rolled in under the portico of their Adelaide Hotel, at around five thirty. Tess went in to reception, got the basket of keys and handed them out to the passengers as they sat on the bus. They were very slow getting off the bus and she felt sorry for them. She was a lot younger than they were and even she was feeling really tired.

'Dinner at six thirty,' she said, 'breakfast goes from seven until nine in the morning. You have a free day tomorrow so you can do whatever you like. I do have some options for you, but I will tell you about them over dinner. Get yourselves into your rooms, have a cuppa and freshen up before dinner.'

Jack was waiting in reception to meet Bill. They were sitting in the lounge together when Tess wheeled her bag in from the bus. She shook hands with Jack and joined the two men for a cold drink.

'We're going back to get the bus,' said Bill.

'Tonight?' Tess was shocked.

'Yes, we can't leave it there overnight, it will likely get stripped.'

Tess looked across at Jack. 'Can't you get anyone else to do it?' asked Tess. 'Bill must be exhausted, aren't you?' She looked at Bill.

'Thanks for your concern Tess but I'll be fine. Jack will be up the front driving the tow vehicle, I will just be following on behind. I might even have a sleep on the way home.'

'You better bloody not mate,' laughed Jack, 'you'll need to be on the ball.'

'I know,' said Bill seriously. 'I'll be fine, honestly, I had a bit of a kip on the bus.'

Jack turned to face Tess. 'Look, I feel bad that the bus broke down on you and I would like to make it up to you in some way. Slim has offered to take your group for a drive out to Glenelg tomorrow if they'd like to go. Or he can drop them off to go shopping somewhere. All at no charge of course.'

Tess was delighted. 'Oh Jack, you don't have

to do that, we've had a fantastic time and the break down was all part of the adventure, us Kiwis tend to take everything in our stride.'

'I can see that,' laughed Jack. 'But the offer is there.'

'I accept, thank you, I will let everyone know at dinner. What time?'

'Whatever time suits you.'

'Let's say ten o'clock then, that will give everyone a chance to have a bit of a sleep in.'

Jack and Bill got up to leave and Tess headed up to her room. A nice long shower was just what she needed.'

Day 14 - A free Day in Adelaide

Slim arrived just before ten the next morning and met Tess at reception.

'How many have we got?' he asked.

'All of them,' laughed Tess. 'I thought some of them might want a day off to themselves but no, they are all keen to cram in another day of sightseeing.'

The group looked remarkably bright and cheerful as they filed out to the van.

'I thought you might all be a bit too tired to do anything more than go for a wander round the shops today,' said Tess as she stood in the doorway of the van.

'It's our last day,' explained June. 'We decided at dinner last night, after you left, that we weren't going to waste it sitting around in a hotel room or going shopping. If there's more to see, then we are all in, isn't that right team?'

Tess laughed at the unanimous response. She looked across at Slim and said, 'Right, Glenelg here we come.' To the group she added, 'We'll just take today as it comes if you like. Maybe have lunch there then see where Slim and the day takes us?' They all nodded in agreement.

There was no sign of the rain from the previous day, it was clear blue skies and sunshine.

As they arrived on the outskirts of Glenelg, Slim started to tell them a little of the history of the area. He pulled up in front of an impressive half round roof structure built over an equally impressive tree that had grown over in a large, perfectly formed arch.

'Glenelg is the oldest European settlement in South Australia,' said Slim proudly. 'At last count there were about thirty-five thousand people living here. This structure here is where a Proclamation was read back on the 28th of December 1836 and it is celebrated here every year on the same date. It's known as the Proclamation of South Australia.'

He drove on around town pointing out some of the beautiful old historic buildings adorning the city. When he arrived at the jetty he asked if anyone wanted to go for a walk. Several of them did so he parked the van and opened the door.

'The jetty is over two hundred metres long,' he cautioned. 'It was originally nearly twice that long when it was first built in 1859. There was a lighthouse at the end of the jetty in those days but unfortunately, in 1873, the lighthouse caught fire and was completely destroyed. Then to top that off, in 1948, a hurricane hit the area and the jetty was completely washed away. All that was left was a kiosk and an aquarium, but they had to be demolished because they had become unsafe. It wasn't until 1969 that the jetty was rebuilt, at only half the length that it was before.'

He left them to wander off up the jetty while he sat on a nearby bench enjoying the sunshine. Just after midday, Slim drove them down to the waterfront and parked close to the cafes and shops where they could get themselves some lunch. As it was midweek, the place was a lot quieter than it would have been if it had been a weekend. They wandered through the souvenir shops searching for gifts to take home, they sat in the sun eating their lunch and watching little children jumping about in a water feature, they meandered along the beautiful Glenelg waterfront and some of them even dipped their toes in the sparkling blue ocean waters. It was the perfect way to wind down after such an adventurous trip. By the time they'd enjoyed a leisurely lunch and a walk around, some of them were beginning to wane. Slim drove them around a few more sights of Adelaide on the way back to the hotel, finally dropping them off at around three o'clock.

'Thank you Slim, this has been a great day. Please say thank you to Jack for me. How did they get on with getting the bus back last night, I forgot to ask.'

'Apparently it was a bit of a hairy drive for Bill as he didn't have any brakes and had to rely on Jack to keep them rolling without needing to come to any sudden stops. I'd say he will be pretty buggered today. Jack said they were both rolling around under that old Hino trying to hook the tow rope on and he'd said to Bill, 'I'm getting too old for this shit. Bill agreed that he was too.'

Tess laughed. 'I didn't get to say goodbye to Bill,' said Tess, 'is there any chance we'll see him before we go?'

'Not sure what he's up to,' said Slim thoughtfully, 'but I will let him know.

'Thanks,' said Tess. 'Have you got a card with the office email address on it, so I can at least send him and Jack an email.'

Slim fished around in his logbook folder and produced a business card.

'Thanks again Slim, it's been great.' She watched him drive off then headed up to her room to get ready for the flight home the next morning.

Around five thirty Tess went down to the bar beside the restaurant to meet up with the group and have a pre-dinner drink, it would be their last meal together. She was surprised and thrilled to see Bill sitting amongst them. He stood when he saw Tess walk in. She walked over and gave him a big hug, tears in her eyes.

'So glad to see you Bill, I wanted to say thank you again for everything you have done for us, this trip wouldn't have been the same without you.' Bill returned her warm hug, he also had tears in his eyes.

'It's been just as good for me too Tess. And you lot,' he glanced around at the group watching on with big smiles on their faces, 'have been the best darn group I have ever taken anywhere, and I mean that with all sincerity.'

Lena stepped forward with an envelope in her hands. 'This is just a little thank you from us Bill, we really enjoyed having you as our driver.'

She handed him the envelope. He opened it and smiled broadly as a group photo with him in it, fell out of the card. He choked up as he started to read the glowing messages of thanks scrawled all over the gaily decorated card.

'Thanks,' he said humbly. Then, pulling himself together, he raised his glass. 'Here's to one of the best outback trips ever and may there be more,' he glanced over at Tess and winked.

Bill joined them for dinner that night. There was a lot of loud chatter and laughter as they recalled details of their epic adventure.

Day 15 – Adelaide to Auckland
– 8th August 2008

A line up of sombre faces greeted Tess when she arrived at breakfast the next morning.

'What's up everyone, why the sad faces?'

'We don't want to go home,' said June sadly, 'we've had such a wonderful time we don't want it to end.'

Tess smiled. 'Well then, why don't we plan another trip. Where would you like to go next?'

There followed a chorus of; 'Cape York', 'Murray River', 'Adelaide to Darwin'.

Tess held up her hand. 'Okay, why don't you write down a list of all the places you want to see, I will go through it and try and come up some trip ideas that cover where most of you want to go.

They brightened up at that prospect and went about finishing their breakfasts and making notes.

'Don't forget your passports,' she advised them as she sat down at the long table with her toast and coffee. 'I've got your tickets, so don't worry about that. And please, go through your carry-on luggage and check you are not taking on board the plane, anything you shouldn't, like food, batteries, lighters, knitting needles, scissors etcetera. Check the list at the airport and do a double check again then, otherwise you will lose whatever they find, it will get tossed in the rubbish bin. The shuttle will be here to pick us up at nine-thirty.'

Back in her room, Tess finished packing her suitcase and hooked her weighing device to the handle. She pulled it up and frowned as the digital readout said twenty-two kilograms. It was heavier than she was comfortable with, she just hoped her small handheld device was accurate and read the same as what the airport machines would read. She took her own advice and double-checked her online luggage. She had packed as much paperwork, booklets and pamphlets as she dared into her suitcase, leaving room in her briefcase for the airline tickets, drop off list, her wallet, a copy of the book 'A Man Called Possum, which Bill had given her, a puzzle book of crossword puzzles, and a jacket that she would probably need when they got home. The day bag she had carted around with her on the trip, along with her cameras, were now packed in her suitcase, hence the extra weight. At least she didn't have to cart too much with her through the airport or on to the plane.

They arrived at the airport at ten o'clock, grabbed some trolleys from a dispenser nearby and trundled their way through to the check-in counters inside. Adelaide airport wasn't big and bustling like Brisbane, Sydney or Melbourne, it was comfortable and accommodating, making their check-in quick and easy and hassle-free. It was a direct flight back to Auckland too, which was a bonus. Tess hated having to break a journey, gather up suitcases and passengers and re-check them in on another flight. It raised her stress-levels somewhat until they were once again in the departure lounge with everyone accounted for.

There were no delays; they boarded Air New Zealand Flight NZ822 and departed within minutes of the scheduled departure time. They landed in Auckland at around six-thirty p.m. and made their way through the duty-free stores to the passport check-in area then down the escalator to pick up their suitcases off the luggage carousel.

Fortuitously, Tess's suitcase was one of the first to appear. She liked to be through the luggage check and out waiting in the arrivals area as people came through so she could gather everyone together. More than once she'd had to race around the large busy airport like a headless chook searching for missing passengers, it was something she didn't need tonight. She made her way through security and went through the self-opening doors into the crowded arrivals lounge looking for her shuttle driver. He spotted her and waved. She pushed her trolley over to him, said hello and turned to see if anyone else from her group was coming through behind her.

'I'm not sure if anyone has come through before me,' she told Arthur, the shuttle driver, 'but I did give them instructions to turn left and look for your sign, hopefully they remember to do that. Coming into a noisy arrivals area with lots of people calling out can be quite confusing.'

'I'm with you on that one Tess,' he said. 'Haven't been many through yet, you'd be one of the first.'

Tess breathed a sigh of relief and, catching Frank and Jan's eye, waved them over to come and stand to one side until the rest of the group joined them.

Tess glanced around and spotted Ahlid holding a sign with June and Aggie's names on it.

'Hello Ahlid,' she said, relived to see him there. 'June and Aggie shouldn't be too long. Are you bringing them back to catch their flight to Christchurch in the morning?'

'I am,' he advised her. 'Don't worry, we will be taking good care of your ladies for you.'

'Thank you,' said Tess, 'I really appreciate that.'

'How was your trip?' Ahlid asked as Aggie and June approached her with their luggage trolleys in tow. 'How about you ask your passengers,' Tess grinned, 'I have no doubt they will be happy to tell you all about it.'

She hugged the lady's goodbye and double-checked they had all the information and paperwork they needed to get them home to Christchurch the next day.

'All set,' confirmed June confidently, 'and thank you for a wonderful trip.'

Aggie grabbed Tess's hand and squeezed it. 'Thank you,' she breathed, 'this might have been my first big trip, but I can guarantee you Tess, it won't be my last. June and I will be looking forward to your next newsletter with the proposed upcoming trips on it. We both want to go back to Australia again.'

'I'm so glad you enjoyed yourself Aggie, perhaps I have unleashed the travel bug in you.'

'I suspect you might have,' agreed June.

They followed Ahlid out to his van and turned at the exit doors to wave goodbye to the gathering group.

Gus and Mandy had caught up with their taxi driver and were saying their goodbyes to the group when Tess re-joined them. They both hugged Tess and told her how much they enjoyed the trip and that they were also looking forward to doing another one again soon.

Finally, everyone was through into the arrivals court, except for Lena.

'Anyone seen Lena?' Tess asked the group. They all shook their heads.

'I think her bag was one of the first to come through on the luggage carousel,' said Jack.

Damn, thought Tess, I wonder where she's got to.

'Where are you parked Arthur?'

'Just out there through those side doors, Roger is waiting there too, with the Rotorua shuttle. Shall I go and get everyone loaded up?'

'Yes please,' said Tess, 'you know who's to go on which shuttle right?'

'Yep, got the list you sent me, we're all good,

you just see if you can find Lena. Here, I'll take your bags for you.'

Tess stood and looked around the arrivals' hall. She went up the escalator leading to the cafes upstairs to get a better look over the crowd below. Nothing. She wandered down past all the check-in counters. Nothing. She was starting to get anxious now, she hated losing passengers, it was her worst nightmare, let alone the fact that it was time consuming and held everyone else up.

'Hope she's okay and that nothing's happened to her,' she thought as she checked the toilet blocks. Despite the fact that it was chilly outside, she decided she might as well check the outside transit area which ran the length of the airport. There sitting on a bench seat as if she was waiting for a bus, was Lena.

'Lena,' Tess was annoyed now. 'What on earth are you doing out here, I have been looking for you everywhere, come on everyone is waiting.'

Lena looked up at Tess. 'I wondered where everyone was,' she smiled, relieved to see a familiar face.

'I told you to turn left when you got into the arrivals lounge,' admonished Tess trying to control her anger.

'Oh, did you?' I don't remember you saying that. I thought we would be picked up where we were dropped off, that's why I came here.'

Tess's anger melted a little. 'Come on let's get out of here,' she said, and steered Lena along the footpath and around the back to the waiting shuttles.

Arthur loaded Lena's suitcase into his van and shut the door. Tess walked back to the Rotorua shuttle, leaned in the door and said goodbye. They decided that a hug was in order, so they climbed back out of the van, hugged Tess and kissed her on the cheek and thanked her for a wonderful trip. The passengers in the front van saw what was happening and did the same. Then they all decided to hug each other, as if it had suddenly dawned on them that they might never see each other again.

Tess had tears in her eyes by the time she'd ushered everyone back in to their respective vans. She waved off the Rotorua shuttle and settled herself in the front seat of the van beside Arthur. She laid her head back on the headrest and closed her eyes and when Arthur asked her how the trip went, she simply said, 'Where do I start?'

Author's Footnote: The group did get to meet up again. In fact, they got together for dinner every year on the anniversary of this trip. They replayed the two-and-a-half-hour video and reminisced about their 'trip of a lifetime'. That was fourteen years ago as this goes to print, I wonder how many of them are still with us.